ENDORSEMENTS

'I am extremely pleased to recommend *The Meaning and Practice of Communion* by Drs. R. K. Beam and R. E. Woods. I have known them both for over half a century and admire them as two of the finest Christian leaders that I have ever worked with in sixty-five years of ministry. They are highly regarded and respected for their devotion, integrity, scholarship, and service in the Lord's church. They have certainly been an inspiration and encouragement to me over the years.

Scores of people have already been blessed, informed, and inspired by their presentations of these communion devotionals in corporate church worship services. Some of them are theological in nature, while others are doctrinal and practical, but all of them can lead to spiritual enrichment and a greater understanding of the Lord's Supper for their readers. They can be used for profit in corporate worship communion service, in private family observance of communion, and simply in personal devotions for one's spiritual well-being."

— DAVID L. EUBANKS, PH.D.
President of Johnson University (1969 - 2007)

"Communion in the Stone-Campbell Movement is practiced so differently in each local congregation. Regrettably, it is either hurried through in the middle of the service, or tacked on at the end, and not much time is given for the congregation to prepare for or participate in it. I had a professor who said, 'We don't celebrate the Supper, we nibble and sip and hurry on our way.' Drs. Beam and Woods, through their scriptural based and well-crafted communion meditations have given the church a tool that will help those leading the communion service to help us slow down and take time to worship the One who said: 'Do this in remembrance of me'. For this purpose, I highly recommend it!"

— LD CAMPBELL
First Church of Christ, Burlington KY.

'In a time of momentary community on social media laden with flashy photos and wisps of pop psychology, the book, *The Meaning and Practice of Communion*, stands in stark contrast and offers wonderful biblical insights. Instead of a long diatribe or exposé, Drs. Bream and Woods bring succinct biblical truth and narrative regarding the very hinge point of faith that is the focus of any worship by Christians.

It is not the 'feel good' songs. It is not the convincing man-delivered sermons; not even the great coffee bars and fellowship meals. It is the God-like practice of communion, which is the pinnacle of any worship. It is the remembrance of the brokenness of humanity—one man at a time coming before a holy God and asking for another chance to love and be loved. This is not convenient—this is a covenant. It is not the Eucharist as 'high church" would define it. This is not simply the Lord's Supper; it is the exchange between humanity and deity.

Drs. Beam and Woods successfully extract nuggets of truth to be pondered on and prayed about during the most intimate time in any worship service—communion. It's been said that to stay relevant in Christianity, one simply has to remember the basics. In this global season of disciple-making movements, micro and private house-church enclaves, and simple fellowships, this poignant book of reflections will find more and more open eyes and hearts as it helps readers and listeners reflect on the one main thing—Christ, the Anointed One, who asked us to 'do and remember.'

The Lord's Supper is a 'comfort food' that you will discover at an entirely new level when reading *The Meaning and Practice of Communion*.

— MIKE SCHRAGE
President, Good News Productions, Int.

THE
MEANING AND PRACTICE OF COMMUNION

104 MEDITATIONS FOR CHURCH AND HOME

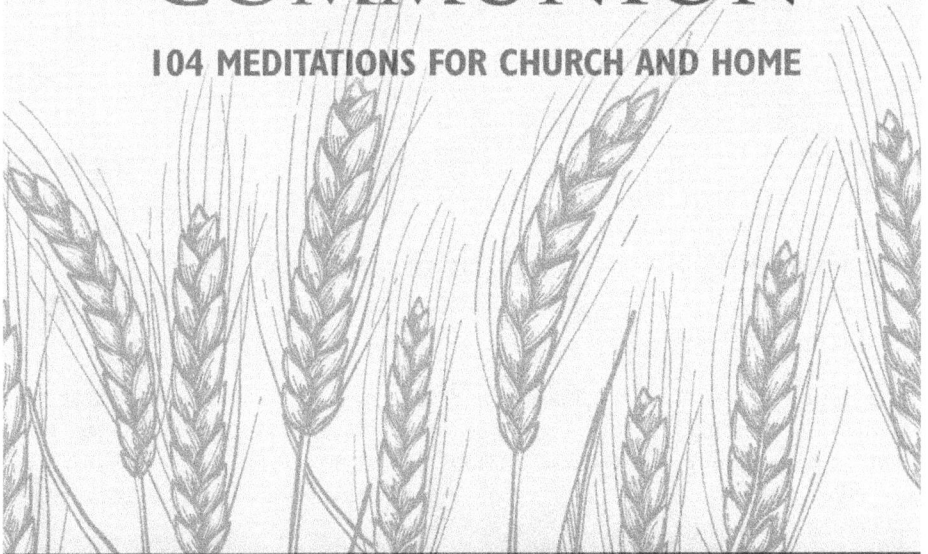

R.K. Beam | R.E. Woods

college press

Joplin, Missouri

ISBN: 978-0-89900-107-4 (paperback)
ISBN: 978-0-89900-109-8 (hardback)
ISBN: 978-0-89900-112-8 (eBook)

CONTENTS

Preface   vii

About the Lord's Supper   1
   Historical Context 1
   Institution 1
   Practice 3
   Meditations 4

The Cost of God's Unmerited Favor   5
  1   A Purposeful Death. 7
  2   A Purposeful Life. 9
  3   Counterbalancing Our Sin. 11
  4   Substitutionary Atonement 13
  5   The Cost of Our Repair. 15
  6   A Costly Mediation 17
  7   Not Saved by Your Belief? 19
  8   The Answer to Everything 21
  9   Look, the Lamb of God 23
 10   The Gift of the Holy Spirit 25
 11   Isaiah 53 27
 12   The Blood of Jesus 31
 13   Counting the Cost 35
 14   Communion Liturgies 37
 15   Do You Fear God? 39
 16   Fulfilling the Law and the Prophets 41

CONTENTS

The Passion of Christ and Culpability of Man   **43**

17   A Suffering Servant 45

18   What's Wrong With This Picture?. 47

19   Suffering Alone 49

20   Scarred Forever 51

21   Discerning God's Will. 55

22   Choices. 57

23   The Blood and the Promise 59

The Purpose of the Lord's Supper   **63**

24   Becoming More Like Jesus 65

25   Examining Our Expectations 67

26   Reinforcing Our Beliefs 71

27   Remembering God's Promises 73

28   The Second Communion 75

29   Celebrating the Death of Jesus 77

30   Remembering the Agony of the Cross 79

31   Proclaiming the Lord's Death 81

32   How to Remember 83

33   Finding the Right Perspective 85

34   Remembering God's Presence 87

35   The Supremacy of Jesus. 89

36   Drawing Close to Christ. 91

37   Remembering Essential Truths 93

38   A Room Called Remember Him 95

39   The Greatness of Jesus 97

The Bread and Cup as Symbols   **99**

40   Ordinary Symbols of Extraordinary Meaning. 101

41   The Bread of Affliction and Cup of Redemption 103

42   The Best of Many 105

43   From the Inside Out 107

44   Beyond Description 109

45   Foreshadowing a Future Banquet 113

46   An Unexpected Pardon 115

CONTENTS

The Art or Practice of Remembering   **117**

47   Communing in Prayer. 119

48   On Being Worthy. 123

49   Worship Lessons 125

50   Communion as Worship. 127

51   The Shadow of the Cup 129

52   Remembered by Jesus. 131

53   Our First Response 133

54   Putting Yourself Ahead of God 135

55   Examining Yourself 137

56   The Hands of Betrayers 139

57   A Comforting Memorial. 141

58   Father, Son, Holy Spirit, and You 143

59   Assessing Your Love of God 145

60   A Fresh Start. 147

61   Unity in Christ 149

62   Rededication 151

The Nature of God   **153**

63   God in the Flesh 155

64   God's Love 157

65   Love in Action 159

66   God's Forgiving Nature 161

67   God's Sternness and Kindness. 163

68   Fully God and Fully Man 165

69   The Joy and Faith of God. 167

70   The Humility of God 169

71   A Mindset of Service 171

72   God's Righteousness 173

73   The Grace of God 175

74   God's Grace and Truth 177

75   God Our Father 179

76   What Would Jesus Do? 181

77   Father Forgive Them 185

78   Remember Me 187

79   Here is Your Son, Here is Your Mother. 189

80   My God, My God, Why? 191

81   I Thirst 193

82   It is Finished 195

83   Into Thy Hands. 197

84   Words From the Cross 199

The Human Predicament   203

85   Worldview 205

86   Reality. 207

87   Culture Wars. 209

88   Understanding Scripture 211

89   The Problem With Individualism 213

90   Some Common Heresies. 215

91   Finding the One Way to God 217

92   Closed Membership and Open Communion 219

93   Self-Centeredness 221

Special Occasions   225

94   A Rescue Mission. 227

95   Married to Christ. 231

96   Our Hope and Peace 233

97   What Child Is This? 235

98   The Adoration of the Christ Child 239

99   Christmas 243

100 Easter 245

101 Thanksgiving. 247

102 New Year's Day 249

103 Independence Day 251

104 Communion for Children 253

Scripture Index   255

PREFACE

There may be no better way to "fix our eyes on Jesus, the author and perfecter of our faith" (Heb 12:2 NIV84), than to think deeply about the cross of Christ. To that end, *The Meaning and Practice of Communion* is a collection of 104 short essays on Christ and His crucifixion.

Each essay is based on a communion meditation that was presented by the authors while presiding at the Lord's Table at the Woodlawn Christian Church in Knoxville, Tennessee. The original meditations have been modified to make them more suitable for personal use. The modifications include: (1) the addition of a *More to Consider* section to spur additional reflection on the subject being discussed, (2) the use of a more formal writing style (e.g., many of the contractions that are typically used when speaking are eliminated), (3) a reorientation of the presentation toward individuals who are reading rather than an audience that is listening, and (4) the removal of Jesus' words of institution[1] when not required to understand the subject under consideration. Despite these changes, each essay maintains its integrity and usefulness as a stand-alone communion mediation for the formal services of the church. When used in that capacity, however, it may be desirable to reinsert the words of institution and employ language that is more suitable for a listening audience and that does not give the impression of an essay being read aloud.

When the meditations of this book were written, there was no intent to publish them, nor was there an established organizational philosophy. Only three—*The Blood and the Promise, Communion in Prayer,* and *The Second Communion*—have previously appeared in print (in issues of Johnson University's *Blue and White* magazine).[2] The impetus to bring them together and create a unified collection of meditations resulted from (1) the desire of some Woodlawn members to use them outside the services of the church, (2) the growing need of post-COVID, online church worshipers to participate in communion from their homes, and (3) from our perception that the centrality of the Lord's Supper in today's worship services is being challenged by the emotional appeal of modern praise and worship music. For the purposes of this book, the included essays are organized into eight basic subject areas:

1. The Cost of God's Unmerited Favor

2. The Passion of Christ and Culpability of Man

3. The Purpose of the Lord's Supper

4. The Bread and Cup as Symbols

5. The Art or Practice of Remembering

6. The Nature of God

7. The Human Predicament

8. Special Occasions

Some essays may touch on more than one area and have been placed where they seemed best to fit. For instance, *God Our Father* is included in the section entitled *The Nature of God* but could have been placed under *Special Occasions* and used as a Father's Day meditation. When this happens, it is noted in the introduction to the area from which it was omitted. Unless otherwise noted, all scripture quotations are taken from the New International Version (NIV) of the Bible. Those from the 1984 edition are referenced as NIV84; other translations are similarly denoted (e.g., NLT for the *New Living Translation*). Abbreviated scripture references follow the recommendations of the *Society of Biblical Literature*.[3]

Drs. Beam and Woods have served as elders of the Woodlawn Christian Church for over two decades. Dr. Beam was the Senior Minister of Woodlawn in the early 1990s. Both have a long association with Johnson

University (formerly Johnson Bible College), whose mission is to educate students for Christian ministries and other strategic vocations framed by the Great Commission in order to extend the kingdom of God among all nations. Both Woodlawn and Johnson trace their roots to the Stone-Campbell Restoration Movement of the early 19th century.[4] (It is the practice of the churches associated with that movement to observe the Lord's Supper weekly.) Dr. Beam is a former Academic Dean of Johnson and Dr. Woods has served on its Board of Trustees for the last 15 years, is the current board chair, and is the author of several books in the field of electrical engineering.

You can learn a lot about Christ and Christianity from a study of the cross of Calvary. Our hope is that this book will help those using it in their homes to do so, and that it will serve as a valuable resource for anyone who is given the honor of presiding over the Lord's Table. In either case, the essays presented should be approached with the humility that the suffering and death of Jesus demands and that is reflected in the following prayer:

> Lord God almighty,
>
> Creator and sustainer of Heaven and earth.
>
> We come to You conscious of our weaknesses and ashamed of our pride.
>
> We have taken You too lightly and taken ourselves too seriously.
>
> We have been offended for ourselves, but insensitive to offenses toward You.
>
> We have been alert to our desires but dull to Your will.
>
> We have worried over food and clothing and shelter, and sought first our kingdom, not Yours.
>
> We have fed our minds with trash and starved our souls.
>
> We have filled our eyes with ugliness and blinded ourselves to your beauty.

And now we come before You as though we deserve your
attention, as though our lives are as clean as our clothes,
and well-fed as our bodies.

Forgive us. Free us of pompousness and pride. Strip us of self-
reliance.

In the name of Jesus, cleanse us from all unrighteousness so
that we may worship and commune with You as Your Son
intended when He first asked us to remember the most
important event in the history of mankind—His atoning
death on the cross.

Amen.

---

[1]See the *Institution* section of the chapter entitled *About the Lord's Supper.*

[2]*Blue and White*, Spring 2005: 7, Spring 2008: 5, and Spring 2010: 4. Meditations 23, 47, and 28, respectively.

[3]*The SBL Handbook of Style*, 2nd ed. (Atlanta: SBL Press, 2014), sections 8.2-8.4.

[4]See Henry Webb, *In Search of Christian Unity: A History of the Restoration Movement* (Abilene, TX: ACU Press, 2003).

[5]Originally published with minor modifications as "A Morning Prayer." Richard Beam, "A Morning Prayer," *Christian Standard*, Nov. 1995: 7.

ABOUT THE
LORD'S SUPPER

NOTHING in a worship service is more Biblical or more important than the Lord's Supper. It is a service of commemoration (Luke 22:19), proclamation (1 Cor 11:26), unification (1 Cor 10:16b, 17), participation (1 Cor 10:16a), and of expectation and consummation (1 Cor 11:26c). Consequently, participating as the leader of a communion service is a humbling honor and serious responsibility. A leader is functioning in the role that Jesus filled in instituting the supper. Likewise, every participant is functioning in the role of an apostle.

The following sections describe the historical context, institution, and practice of communion from its inception to today.

HISTORICAL CONTEXT

Communion, also called the Lord's Supper or the Eucharist, grew out of a Jewish practice called the Passover Feast. When the Jews were preparing for their Exodus from Egypt, God instructed them to prepare and eat a meal that was to become a memorial to their deliverance from Egyptian slavery (Exod 12). The meal was called the Passover meal and Jews have kept it faithfully to this day.

INSTITUTION

In the last days of his life, Jesus, being a Jew, observed the Passover together with His Apostles. At the end of the meal, He gave it new meaning—or revealed its real meaning—by instituting the Lord's Supper. He instructed

1

His followers to observe the Supper in remembrance of Him. With respect to Jesus' words of institution, the narratives of Matthew, Mark, and Luke are similar. Matthew writes:

> While they were eating, Jesus took bread, and when he had given thanks, he broke it and gave it to his disciples, saying, "Take and eat; this is my body."
>
> Then he took a cup, and when he had given thanks, he gave it to them, saying, "Drink from it, all of you. This is my blood of the covenant, which is poured out for many for the forgiveness of sins. I tell you, I will not drink from this fruit of the vine from now on until that day when I drink it new with you in my Father's kingdom."
>
> When they had sung a hymn, they went out to the Mount of Olives. (Matt 26:27-30)

Like Matthew, Mark equates the bread and cup to Jesus' body and blood, recording the institution of the Lord's Supper as follows:

> While they were eating, Jesus took bread, and when he had given thanks, he broke it and gave it to his disciples, saying, "Take it; this is my body."
>
> Then he took a cup, and when he had given thanks, he gave it to them, and they all drank from it.
>
> "This is my blood of the covenant, which is poured out for many," he said to them. (Mark 14:22-24)

The most notable difference between the accounts of Matthew, Mark, and Luke is Luke's addition of the statement *do this in remembrance of me*:

> When the hour came, Jesus and his apostles reclined at the table. And he said to them, "I have eagerly desired to eat this Passover with you before I suffer. For I tell you, I will not eat it again until it finds fulfillment in the kingdom of God." After taking the cup, he gave thanks and said, "Take this and divide it among you. For I tell you I will not drink again from the fruit of the vine until the

2

kingdom of God comes."

And he took bread, gave thanks and broke it, and gave it to them, saying, "This is my body given for you; do this in remembrance of me."   (Luke 22:14-19)

In addition to these passages on the institution of the Lord's Supper, the practice is later reiterated and expanded upon in 1 Corinthians 10-11, where Paul addresses the way believers should approach communion. Paul's instructions are considered one of the principal biblical texts on communion.

PRACTICE

Except for 1 Corinthians 11, where Paul addresses the abuses of the Lord's Supper by the Corinthian church, there is no Biblical command or precedent regarding how the church is to observe the Lord's Supper. As a result, there is little uniformity across the Christian world with respect to its practice, and there has been some controversy. Some churches are very formal or liturgical (following a prescribed set of rituals); others are informal. Some observe the Lord's Supper monthly or quarterly, others weekly. Among those, like Christian Churches and Churches of Christ, who observe the Supper informally and weekly, the method of observance varies by congregation and perhaps by region. Some churches pass the bread first and eat it together; then they pass the cup and drink it together under the instruction of the leader. Some use one cup; others many little cups. Some use a separate tray for the bread and cup; others use one. Likewise, the emblems may vary from grape juice to wine and from bread to crackers. Almost always there is a hymn, scripture reading including the words of institution, prayer, and a meditation. Consequently, procedures for observing the Lord's Supper are somewhat arbitrary. You may wonder why your church observes the supper in one way and not another. The answer is: that is the way they have chosen to do it at your church.

It has been the practice of Christian Churches of the Stone-Campbell Movement, following Scriptural precedent (Acts 20:7), to observe the Lord's Supper weekly. Others observe it less frequently.

MEDITATIONS

The meditation should be focused on some aspect of the meaning of the Lord's Supper. The meaning of the Lord's Supper encompasses everything from the birth to the glorious return of Christ, so the meditation may have a range of topics and tones, but it should never be frivolous or folksy. Here are some tips for the communion meditation.

- The meditation does not need a lengthy introduction. The service up to this sacred moment should have served to prepare the people for the communion.

- With few exceptions (say Christmas or Easter), the meditation need not attempt to make the communion relevant to the activities of life like sports or politics. The meaning of the communion is timeless and next to it nearly all else is frivolous.

- The meditation should not be a general devotional with the meaning of the Lord's Supper artificially attached.

- The meditation should not seek novelty. It is the least important aspect of the communion service and should not detract from the Scripture, prayer, bread, and cup. The communion would have eternal meaning without the meditation, but the meditation may enhance the understanding and the experience of the congregation if presented carefully, thoughtfully, and reverently.

- The meditation should in no way call attention to the one speaking, but rather should draw attention to Christ and Him alone.

THE COST OF
GOD'S UNMERITED FAVOR

1   A Purposeful Death 7

2   A Purposeful Life. 9

3   Counterbalancing Our Sin. 11

4   Substitutionary Atonement 13

5   The Cost of Our Repair. 15

6   A Costly Mediation 17

7   Not Saved by Your Belief? 19

8   The Answer to Everything 21

9   Look, the Lamb of God 23

10   The Gift of the Holy Spirit 25

11   Isaiah 53 27

12   The Blood of Jesus 31

13   Counting the Cost 35

14   Communion Liturgies. 37

15   Do You Fear God? 39

16   Fulfilling the Law and the Prophets 41

THE IMPORTANCE OF JESUS' DEATH cannot be overstated. It is the cost of God's unmerited favor, the price of the grace and forgiveness that all Christians depend upon. Though we are ultimately responsible for Jesus' death (it would not have been necessary if man had not sinned), we did not select the conditions under which

God would forgive us. To be true to Himself and make creation what He intended, the death of His Son was a requirement of His Holy nature. It is impossible for us to completely understand why Jesus had to die, but there are several ways that we can think about it. The 16 meditations in this section explore some of those ways. The first meditation, for example, presents the four principal arguments that are made by the writers of the New Testament—that Jesus' death (1) satisfied God's anger over our sin, (2) purchased our freedom from slavery to sin, (3) paid the penalty for our crimes against God, and (4) mended our relationship with Him. The remaining meditations focus on one or more of these ideas or simply remind us that the suffering and death of Jesus is indeed the cost of our salvation.

1

A PURPOSEFUL DEATH

COMMUNION focuses our attention on the physical death of Jesus and the related question: *Why did He have to die on a cross?* Because the success of the early church, at least in part, depended on the answer to that question, the writers of the New Testament gave us several ways to think about the purpose of Jesus' death.

They wrote, for instance, that because of Jesus' death, we are "saved from God's wrath" (Rom 5:9). That is, on the cross, the crucified Jesus bore the brunt of God's anger over our sin. His death was a work of *propitiation* or appeasement.

They wrote that Jesus "gave himself to redeem us from all wickedness" (Titus 2:14) and remove our fear of death.[1] If you picture yourself as a slave to sin and death, Jesus forfeited His life to put an end to your bondage. So, His death was a work of *redemption* as well as one of propitiation.

They wrote that Jesus is "the atoning sacrifice for our sins" (1 John 2:2). In a court of law, His death would be considered reparation for our crimes against God—a work of atonement, often called *substitutionary atonement.*

And they wrote that we are "reconciled to God through the death of his Son" (Rom 5:8). On the cross, we see the extent of God's love for us and, as a result, we earnestly desire a relationship with Him. That is a prerequisite—maybe the only prerequisite—for God to break down the barrier created by our sin and make us holy in His sight. Jesus' death was not only a work of propitiation and redemption and atonement, but a work of *reconciliation* as well.

Jesus simply described the purpose of His death in this way:

> **This is my blood of the covenant which is poured out for many for the forgiveness of sins.** (Matt 26:28)

The term propitiation places the focus of that *forgiveness* on the removal of God's wrath. Redemption places the focus on freeing us from sin's bondage. Atonement places the focus on paying the penalty for our disobedience. And reconciliation places the focus on repairing our relationship with God.

So, when you take the bread and cup of communion, think about the broken, bleeding body[2] of God's Son—who endured the wrath, who paid the ransom that freed us from sin's bondage, who suffered the punishment that was warranted by our disobedience, and who ultimately mended our relationship with God.

PRAYER

Father, it is to our great benefit that through the obedience of Jesus we are made righteous.[3] We are grateful for the purposeful death that He endured on our behalf, and we thank you for it in Jesus' name. Amen.

MORE TO CONSIDER

In your personal experiences, have there been occasions when one or more of these four aspects of forgiveness was demonstrated on a human level? Are any of them unique to God alone?

---

[1]See Heb 2:15.

[2]Jesus' body was bruised, battered, flogged, pierced, and nailed to a cross, but as prophesied in Psalm 34:20, his bones were not broken (see John 19:28-34). The adjective "broken" is used here and throughout the book to connote "weakened in strength, spirit, etc."

[3]See Rom 5:19.

2

A PURPOSEFUL LIFE

H E WAS BORN AS GOD AMONG MEN. He was God become flesh, full of grace and truth. He was the great "I am," God Himself. What He did and said was from God. Even though the Bible does not tell us to do so, we celebrate His coming into our world once a year at Christmas—the coming of Jesus, the coming of God. God has come among us to experience what it is to be human and to show us what God is like.

Wow, God became man. It is hard to imagine anything more significant than God becoming man.

But there is more. In a reality that is almost too good to be true, Jesus arose from the dead. He was killed by His enemies in an ugly and gruesome way. He was clearly and unquestionably dead. He was in the grave for three days. But when His friends came to perform burial rights, He was gone. He appeared alive to 11 apostles and to as many as 500 people at one time over a period of 40 days before He ascended into the heavens. Even though there is no Biblical requirement to do so, we celebrate this resurrection reality once a year at Easter.

Wow, death is not the end. It is hard to imagine anything more significant than resurrection.

But there is more. The rest is so important that we celebrate it not each year but each week at the Lord's Table, and we do it not out of tradition, but at the instruction of Jesus. The apostle Paul wrote:

For whenever you eat this bread and drink this cup, you proclaim the Lord's death until he comes. (1 Cor 11:26)

We do this following the example of the Apostles who, it could be argued, met on the first day of the week for this purpose.

It is impossible to separate these events in the life of Christ—His coming as God in the flesh and His bodily resurrection—but the thing He asked us to memorialize is this: He died for our sins. The death of Jesus works for the forgiveness of the sins of those who accept it. His coming into the world made it all possible. His resurrection proved it was all true.

Wow, our sins have been forgiven. We celebrate that truth every week around the Lord's Table. It is hard to imagine anything more significant than the forgiveness of sins, because for us there is nothing more significant.

PRAYER

We thank you, our Father, for the forgiveness of sin that is made possible by the life and death of Jesus. We remember His purposeful life and crucified body as we worship you in His name. Amen.

MORE TO CONSIDER

Do isolated events in Jesus' life make any sense without considering His entire life? Though He specifically asked us to remember His death, would it make any sense without the incarnation, a life without sin, or the resurrection?

3

COUNTERBALANCING OUR SIN

I MAGINE THIS. Suppose that you have a device for measuring sin—the spiritual equivalent of an old-fashioned balance scale. And imagine putting the sin of the world on one side of the scale:

- Include the greed, lust, envy, pride, hatred, and selfishness of all 117 billion people who are thought to have inhabited the earth.[1]

- Include the atrocities committed during the Holocaust and 911 and add the over 60 million legalized abortions since Roe v. Wade.[2]

- Include the sin of the people of Noah's generation, whose hearts, God said, were filled with evil all the time.[3]

- Put Judas' betrayal of Jesus on the scale, and Peter's denial of Him as well.

- And then add your own sin too.

Imagining the sin of the world is like counting the stars in the universe. It makes you wonder if there is anything that can be placed on the other side of the scale to counterbalance all that sin.

Fortunately for us, God has provided what it takes. When John the Baptist called Jesus "the Lamb of God" (John 1:29), he was revealing what it takes:

11

- It takes the equivalent of an Old Testament Passover Lamb, but one that can atone for billions and billions of sinners.

- It takes something like the scapegoat used on the Day of Atonement in Leviticus,[4] but one that can carry away unlimited sin.

- In the context of the Lord's Supper, it takes the sacrificial death of arguably the rarest and thus most valuable thing in the created universe—a man without sin, a lamb without blemish or defect.

In the words of John the Baptist, to take away the sin of the world, it takes "the Lamb of God" (John 1:29), the Lamb who is God, our Lord and Savior Jesus Christ.

PRAYER

Father, we know that man's sin is great and ever increasing. We also know that people respond to their sin in different ways—that there is an important difference between Judas' betrayal of Jesus and Peter's denial of Him. And it is not the severity of their sin, but their repentance. So, as sinners who want the sacrifice of Jesus to work in our lives and take away our sin, we thank you for the body and blood that was broken and poured out for us. And we are grateful for the grace that it provides for all who earnestly follow Jesus. Amen.

MORE TO CONSIDER

Like the number of stars in the universe, the sin of man is seemingly infinite and beyond our comprehension. Consider the most valuable thing that you could contribute to offset sin of such magnitude. Can you imagine God sacrificing anything more valuable than His one and only Son?

---

[1] Toshiko Kaneda and Carl Haub, "How Many People Have Ever Lived on Earth,?" *Population Reference Bureau*, April 2021, prb.org/articles/how-many-people-have-ever-lived-on-earth/.

[2] See "Number of Abortions – Abortion Counters," *numberofabortions.com*, January, 2022, http://www.numberofabortions.com/.

[3] See Gen 6:5.

[4] See Lev 16:8-10.

4

SUBSTITUTIONARY ATONEMENT

I T IS HARD TO READ the 53rd chapter of Isaiah without getting the point. It is made at least a dozen times—sometimes figuratively, other times more directly. In the middle stanza of the five-stanza song, Isaiah mentions it seven times (*italicized* in the following verses):

> Surely *he took up our pain* and *bore our suffering,* yet we considered him punished by God, stricken by him, and afflicted.
> But *he was pierced for our transgressions, he was crushed for our iniquities;*
> *the punishment that brought us peace was on him,* and *by his wounds we are healed.*
> We all, like sheep, have gone astray, each of us has turned to our own way;
> and *the Lord has laid on him the iniquity of us all.*   (Isa 53:4-6)

The point is, of course, that Jesus took our place—when we needed it most—suffering instead of us and paying for our sins.

The writers of the New Testament got it. They made the 53rd chapter of Isaiah the most frequently quoted passage of the Old Testament. They saw how Jesus suffered and how He died. They knew He had done nothing wrong. And they witnessed His life, and teaching, and miracles, and

13

resurrection. After experiencing all of that, Peter paraphrased Isaiah's writing in 1st Peter Chapter 2, and explained it in light of what he had learned from Jesus in this way:

> He himself [*meaning Jesus*] bore our sins in his body on the tree, so that we might die to sins and live for righteousness; by his wounds you have been healed. (1 Pet 2:24)

PRAYER

Father, we remember now the sacrifice of your Son, whose body was broken and whose blood was poured out for us. He paid the penalty that we ourselves— because of our sin—could not pay. We are thankful for the grace that comes through His willingness to bear our iniquity. May we now, as a result, live for righteousness. Amen.

MORE TO CONSIDER

Can you think of a time when you willingly accepted the blame for the wrongdoings of another? If the punishment had been death, would you still have accepted the blame? If so, what would you have expected in return? What should God expect in return?

5

THE COST
OF OUR REPAIR

IN TODAY'S ECONOMY, FEWER and fewer things are worth the cost of their repair. If someone accidentally drops a cell phone and breaks it, they will more than likely throw it away and get a new one. Should a building require substantial renovation, it is frequently cheaper to tear it down and build a new one. If you assume, as is our natural tendency, that God spoke the universe into existence at little or no personal cost, conventional wisdom suggests that He would refuse to commit significant resources to the repair of a broken universe. But the crucifixion of His Son defies that kind of reasoning:

- God created a world in which He could be loved *without coercion.*

- Where things can be simple or so complex that we can't understand them.

- Where both order and chaos surround us.

- And where we are forced to make decisions in the presence of complexity and uncertainty and even deceit.

And when we failed in that environment, when Adam and Eve disobeyed God and the question arose, 'Should I destroy these disobedient people and begin again, or bear the cost of their repair?", God chose to fix us. "God so loved the world that he gave his one and only Son" (John 3:16) to fix us. In fact, the life and death of Jesus would fix more than just us. The author of Romans suggests that it is the cost of all creation's repair. The NLT says it this way:

> All creation anticipates the day when it will join God's children in glorious freedom from death and decay. For we know that all creation has been groaning as in the pains of childbirth right up to the present time. (Rom 8:21–22 NLT)

When in the process of taking communion, we remember the words: "my body given for you... my blood, which is poured out for you" (Luke 22:19–20), the loaf and the cup should remind us that:

1. The body and blood of Jesus were sacrificed to enable people to follow God freely.

2. And that in God's mind, it is more just and desirable to repair a broken universe containing broken people than to destroy both and begin again.

PRAYER

Father, we are grateful that you chose to fix us—that Jesus gave His life for our repair. Rather than discarding us as defective, our failures became yet another reason for us to love you, which is what you wanted from the moment of creation. We pray that we will return to you that which you so desire, and that we will never forget the sacrifice of both you and your Son. Amen.

MORE TO CONSIDER

Have you ever felt beyond repair? In what ways do you think that all creation is groaning?

6

A Costly Mediation

A s Christians, we believe that the moment Jesus died something miraculous happened. Matthew 27:51 says:

At that moment the curtain of the temple was torn from top to bottom. The earth shook and the rocks split.   (Matt 27:51)

The author of Hebrews wrote that because of that moment:

. . . we have confidence to enter the Most Holy Place [*meaning the presence of God*] by the blood of Jesus, by a new and living way opened for us through the curtain, that is, his body ...   (Heb 10:19-20)

Upon Jesus' death, He became "the mediator of a new covenant" (Heb 9:15), the sole arbiter between God and us. It is not easy to understand how a death could do that, but it surely has something to do with the fact that Jesus and Jesus alone is both fully God and fully human. The New Testament tells us that He had to be made like us in every way so that He could become a "merciful and faithful high priest in service to God" (Heb 2:17). According to C. S. Lewis, it tells us that "Christ was killed for us, that His death has washed out our sin, and that by dying He disabled death itself."[1] That, in a nutshell, is Christianity. It is what we believe. And it is what we pause to remember when we take the Lord's Supper.

17

According to Luke, on the night before Jesus was crucified, He took some bread and wine and said to the apostles:

> This is my body given for you; do this in remembrance of me. . . This cup is the new covenant in my blood, which is poured out for you.
>
> (Luke 22:14-20)

And so, we remember:

> For there is one God and one mediator between God and man, the man Christ Jesus, who gave himself as a ransom for all people.
>
> (1 Tim 2:5-6)

PRAYER

Our Heavenly Father, we are a people who have been prone to sin from birth. We desperately need to be reconciled with you, and we are incapable of accomplishing that on our own. So, we thank you for Jesus, who endured the cross, established a new covenant, and became our merciful and faithful high priest, a gracious and dependable mediator between us, as fallen creatures, and you, as our righteous creator. Amen.

MORE TO CONSIDER

Why do you need a mediator with God? What qualities of Jesus make Him the ideal candidate to intercede for man?

---

[1]C. S. Lewis, *Mere Christianity* (New York: Simon & Schuster, 1996), 59.

7

NOT SAVED
BY YOUR BELIEF?

I BELIEVE that Jesus is the Christ, the Son of the living God, but I am not saved by that belief. To quote James, the brother of Jesus:

Even the demons believe that—and shudder. (Jas 2:19)

No one can lead a sinless life—only Jesus could—and I am sorry when I disappoint God, but feelings of sorrow and repentance do not save me. They mainly reveal that I want to be saved. Being submersed in a body of water, on its own, could not have saved me. And while I try to obey the teachings of Jesus, even obedience cannot save me. Obeying the law did not work before Jesus came into the world, and it was not the solution He brought to the world.

Despite their importance, it is not belief, repentance, baptism, or obedience that make me right with God. As Oswald Chambers once wrote, 'I am made right with God... because prior to all of that, Christ died.'[1] The road we travel to salvation, the ease or difficulty of the journey, whether we experience a gradual turning over of our lives to Christ or a more sudden and dramatic one, all those things and more are secondary matters. Without Jesus' death, belief, repentance, baptism, and obedience lose their effectiveness and all the religious experiences and good works in

19

the world would not save us.

When we take the Lord's Supper, we remember the only thing that can atone for sin and make each of us holy before God—the broken body and the shed blood of His one and only Son.

PRAYER

Our Father, we often give ourselves more credit than we deserve. And when it comes to our salvation, we deserve little if any credit. It is not about us and what we have done, but about Jesus and what He did on the cross. The bread and cup of communion always remind us of Him and His great sacrifice on our behalf and for our salvation. Amen.

MORE TO CONSIDER

In what ways have you tried to earn your salvation? If God were to ask you why you should be saved, what would your answer be?

---

[1]Oswald Chambers, "Justification by Faith," in *My Utmost for His Highest: An Updated Edition in Today's Language*, ed. James Reimann (Grand Rapids, MI: Discovery House Publishers, 2017), Day October 28.

8

THE ANSWER
TO EVERYTHING

I T HAS BEEN SUGGESTED that in the epistles of Paul, the cross is offered as the solution to every problem that Paul addresses.[1] Consider the following questions and answers from Paul's writing.

Is there division in the church? The answer is found in the cross:

> Is Christ divided? Was Paul crucified for you?   (1 Cor 1:13)

Does someone have a bad attitude?

> Your attitude should be the same as that of Christ Jesus: Who .... humbled himself and became obedient to death—even death on a cross!   (Phil 2:5, 8 NIV84)

What does God consider to be wisdom?

> For the message of the cross is foolishness to those who are perishing, but to us who are being saved it is the power of God. For it is written: "I will destroy the wisdom of the wise; the intelligence of the intelligent I will frustrate."   (1 Cor 1:18-19)

Do we have anything to brag about as Christians?

> May I never boast except in the cross of our Lord Jesus Christ, through which the world has been crucified to me, and I to the world.   (Gal 6:14)

Because of our sin, we made ourselves enemies of God, but Jesus made God accessible again. How did He do that?

> For God was pleased to have all his fullness dwell in him, and through him to reconcile to himself all things, whether things on earth or things in heaven, by making peace through his blood, shed on the cross. (Col 1:19-20)

How shall we think of the change that has taken place in our lives because of Christ? Paul says it this way:

> For we know that our old self was crucified with him so that the body of sin might be done away with, and that we should no longer be slaves to sin—because anyone who has died has been freed from sin. (Rom 6:6-7)

> I have been crucified with Christ and I no longer live, but Christ lives in me. (Gal 2:20)

> Those who belong to Christ Jesus have crucified the sinful nature with its passions and desires. (Gal 5:24)

How shall we look to the future?

> Let us fix our eyes on Jesus, the author and perfecter of our faith, who for the joy set before him endured the cross, scorning its shame, and sat down at the right hand of the throne of God. (Heb 12:2 NIV84)

These verses are, among other things, what the death of Jesus means.

Prayer

Our Father in Heaven, of all the things we give you thanks, the one that makes least sense to the world is the cross. It is foolishness to them, but it is the power of God unto salvation for us, and for that we thank you and remember the broken body and shed blood of Jesus. Amen.

More to Consider

Are there meaningful questions in life that the cross is not the answer to?

---

[1]Rick Atchley, the minister of one of the largest non-instrumental Churches of Christ in America, made this observation during one of the Gilmore-Sanders Lectures. "Gilmore-Sanders Lectures," presented by Rick Atchley, Johnson University, Knoxville, TN, October, 2005.

9

Look, the Lamb of God

I N THE OPENING chapter of the book of John, John the Baptist sees Jesus approaching the Jordan River and says to the crowd around him:

Look, the Lamb of God who takes away the sin of the world.
(John 1:29)

Think about that. It was amazing news, but as it turns out, no one understood it. More than likely, John himself did not understand the full implications. And if we had been there that day, we would not have either. The term *Lamb of God* was new to everyone. It is not found in the Law or the Prophets or the Psalms. Its meaning must be inferred from them:

- From Old Testament statutes in which lambs are used as sin and guilt offerings.[1]

- From the saving power of the blood of a lamb without blemish in the Exodus from Egypt.[2]

- From Abraham's claim, when asked to sacrifice his only son, that 'God himself will provide the lamb for the burnt offering" (Gen 22:8).

The faithful of Israel laid their hands on lamb after lamb, as if to transfer their sin to innocent animals, and then slaughtered them to atone for their transgressions. But not until after the resurrection could Jesus' own apostles put two and two together and see Him as the ultimate sacrificial lamb. Jesus, of course, knew exactly what it meant to be the Lamb of God:

- He knew what it meant when He said "This is my body given for you... This cup is the new covenant in my blood, which is poured out for you" (Luke 22:20).

- He knew what it meant when He studied Isaiah's prophesy that He would be "led like a lamb to the slaughter" (Isa 53:7).

And today, we too know what it means:

- The bread and cup of communion are the body and blood of the Lamb of God.

- Jesus is the lamb "who takes away the sin of the world" (John 1:29).

- And we are the recipients of an amazing grace that flows from His once-and-for-all sacrifice as the Lamb of God.

PRAYER

Father, "Worthy is the Lamb, who was slain, to receive power and wealth and wisdom and strength and honor and glory and [our] praise" (Rev 5:12). Amen.

MORE TO CONSIDER

It has been estimated that 250,000 sheep were needed every year for Passover sacrifices and the accompanying feast. What was the ultimate purpose of all that bloodshed?

---

[1]See, for example, Lev 4.

[2]See Exod 12.

10

THE GIFT OF
THE HOLY SPIRIT

Y OU PROBABLY KNOW the words by heart, can picture the place—the upper room—in your mind. Jesus gives the bread and cup of the Passover meal to the apostles and says: "This is my body given for you... This cup is the new covenant in my blood, which is poured out for you" (Luke 22:19-20). What transpired that evening, though not normally thought of in this way, was prophetic, because:

- Jesus gave Himself *for us* on the following day.

- And gave Himself *to us* when we later gave ourselves to Him.

In the Sermon on the Mount, Jesus said, "Do not think that I have come to abolish the Law or the Prophets; I have not come to abolish them but to fulfill them" (Matt 5:17). The covenant that Jesus died to establish was not about abolishing old laws or setting less stringent standards for righteousness; it was about changing our character so that we can follow God's law. Five hundred years earlier, the prophet Jeremiah recorded this promise of the new covenant: "I will put my law in their minds and write it on their hearts" (Jer 31:33). Ezekiel, a fellow prophet, revealed how that would be done: "I will put My Spirit in you," God said, "and move you to follow my decrees" (Ezek 36:27). Jesus, in concert with the Father, fulfills that New Covenant promise by sending His Holy Spirit to us. So:

- Remember again that Jesus gave Himself *for us* on Calvary, atoning for our sin, purchasing God's forgiveness, and setting things right between God and us.

- Remember that He gave Himself *to us* in Spirit, instilling in our hearts and minds the desire, and strength, to follow God's law—to gradually become like Him.

- And remember that for the New Covenant to work as God intended, we need both—His forgiveness and His Spirit.

PRAYER

Father, we in no way deserve it. Jesus gave Himself for us on a cross and gave Himself to us in Spirit. He paid for our sin and works within us as we strive to follow Him. Help us each to do that faithfully. I pray in His name, Amen.

MORE TO CONSIDER

Can you sense the presence of the Holy Spirit in your life? How has the Spirit changed you?

11

ISAIAH 53

APPROXIMATELY 700 YEARS BEFORE the crucifixion of Jesus, Isaiah wrote these famous words about the purpose of His death.

Who has believed our message
and to whom has the arm of the Lord been revealed?

He grew up before him like a tender shoot,
and like a root out of dry ground.
He had no beauty or majesty to attract us to him,
nothing in his appearance that we should desire him.

He was despised and rejected by mankind,
a man of suffering, and familiar with pain.
Like one from whom people hide their faces,
he was despised, and we held him in low esteem.

Surely he took up our pain
and bore our suffering,
yet we considered him punished by God,
stricken by him, and afflicted.

But he was pierced for our transgressions,
he was crushed for our iniquities;

the punishment that brought us peace was on him,
    and by his wounds we are healed.

We all, like sheep, have gone astray,
    each of us has turned to our own way;
and the Lord has laid on him
    the iniquity of us all.

He was oppressed and afflicted,
    yet he did not open his mouth;
he was led like a lamb to the slaughter,
    and as a sheep before her shearers is silent,
    so he did not open his mouth.

By oppression and judgment he was taken away.
    Yet who of his generation protested?
For he was cut off from the land of the living;
    for the transgressions of my people he was punished.

He was assigned a grave with the wicked,
    and with the rich in his death,
though he had done no violence,
    nor was any deceit in his mouth.

Yet it was the Lord's will to crush him and cause him to suffer,
    and though the Lord makes his life an offering for sin,
he will see his offspring and prolong his days,
    and the will of the Lord will prosper in his hand.

After he has suffered,
    he will see the light of life and be satisfied;
by his knowledge my righteous servant will justify many,
    and he will bear their iniquities.

Therefore I will give him a portion among the great,
    and he will divide the spoils with the strong,
because he poured out his life unto death,
    and was numbered with the transgressors.

> For he bore the sin of many,
>   and made intercession for the transgressors.

We, of course, are among those He suffered and died for.

PRAYER

Our Father, as we take the bread and the cup, Isaiah reminds us that Jesus was indeed "led like a lamb to the slaughter." He was "pierced for our transgressions," and "made intercession for [*us*] the transgressors." Isaiah's message is clear. His words speak for themselves. And we are thankful that they are no longer an unfulfilled prophecy. Amen.

MORE TO CONSIDER

The writers of the New Testament quoted this chapter of Isaiah more than any other Old Testament scripture. Which of its prophecies are said to be fulfilled by Jesus? Are there any unfulfilled prophesies in the passage?

12

The Blood of Jesus

Since we have now been justified by his blood, how much more shall we be saved from God's wrath through him! (Rom 5:9)

In him we have redemption through his blood, the forgiveness of sins, in accordance with the riches of God's grace... (Eph 1:7)

HOW ARE WE TO UNDERSTAND the references to the blood of Christ in these two passages? Are we to think that there is something magical in His blood? A superficial look at such hymns as *There is Power in the Blood* and *Are You Washed in the Blood* might give that impression. One even claims, "There is a Fountain filled with blood drawn from Immanuel's veins." How are we to understand such references to the blood of Jesus?

There is a figure of speech in English called a *metonymy*. It is the use of the name of one object or concept for that of another to which it is related. For example, if you were to receive a telephone call saying, "This is the White House calling," you would obviously know that houses do not call and talk to people, but that a representative of the president's administration is calling on official government business. In this case, White House equals the president's representative. In the same way, when the New Testament speaks of the blood of Jesus, it is a metonymy with

31

"blood" referring to the death of Jesus on the Cross. It is referring to the time and place when He shed his blood for the remission of sin.

With that in mind, consider the following passages and read the word "blood" to be the death of Jesus on the cross:

> Since we have now been justified by his blood [*the death of Jesus on the cross*], how much more shall we be saved from God's wrath through him! (Rom 5:9)

> In him we have redemption through his blood [*the death of Jesus on the cross*], the forgiveness of sins, in accordance with the riches of God's grace. (Eph 1:7)

> But if we walk in the light, as he is in the light, we have fellowship with one another, and the blood of Jesus [*the death of Jesus on the cross*], his Son, purifies us from all sin. (1 John 1:7)

> But now in Christ Jesus you who once were far away have been brought near by the blood of Christ [*the death of Jesus on the cross*]. (Eph 2:13)

> Keep watch over yourselves and all the flock of which the Holy Spirit has made you overseers. Be shepherds of the church of God, which he bought with his own blood [*the death of Jesus on the cross*]. (Acts 20:28)

> How much more, then, will the blood of Christ [*the death of Jesus on the cross*], who through the eternal Spirit offered himself unblemished to God, cleanse our consciences from acts that lead to death, so that we may serve the living God! (Heb 9:14)

> For you know that it was not with perishable things such as silver or gold that you were redeemed from the empty way of life handed down to you from your ancestors, but with the precious blood of Christ [*the death of Jesus on the cross*], a lamb without blemish or defect. He was chosen before the creation of the world, but was revealed in these last times for your sake. (1 Pet 1:18-20)

As we remember the blood of Jesus and all that it means, reflect on these words of the Apostle Paul:

> Is not the cup of thanksgiving for which we give thanks a participation in the blood of Christ? And is not the bread that we break a participation in the body of Christ? (1 Cor 10:16)

PRAYER

Father, we have not the capacity to properly thank you for the blood of Christ, which He shed, spilled, poured out, emptied on our behalf. But following His instruction, we pause to remember and to participate in His blood and His body. Amen.

MORE TO CONSIDER

According to the passages listed above, what has the death of Jesus on the cross done for you?

13

COUNTING THE COST

I F YOU BELIEVE that God is all-knowing, that His knowledge is both infinite and effortless, then it does not make sense to think that He was surprised when Adam and Eve sinned or for that matter, when you or I have. If God knows everything—the past and present and future—then the crucifixion of His Son cannot be a spur-of-the-moment solution to an unanticipated problem.

The sacrifice we remember around the Lord's Table—the "giving" that is referred to in John 3:16—is at the center of God's plan for us and the world:

- He created people who could choose to disobey Him.

- Knowing they would disobey.

- And that the body and blood of His Son would purchase their passage into a new heaven and a new earth that were the objective from the start.

We do not normally think about it in this way, but God so loved the world that He created it knowing that Jesus would suffer and die so that sinful people like us could learn to follow Him freely and be transformed into sinless people who could live with Him forever.

On the back of the book *3:16 The Numbers of Hope*[1] by Max Lucado, the words of John 3:16 are arranged in this familiar shape:

FOR GOD
SO LOVED
THE WORLD
THAT HE
GAVE HIS
ONE AND ONLY SON
THAT
WHOEVER
BELIEVES
IN HIM
SHALL NOT
PERISH
BUT HAVE
ETERNAL
LIFE.
JOHN 3:16

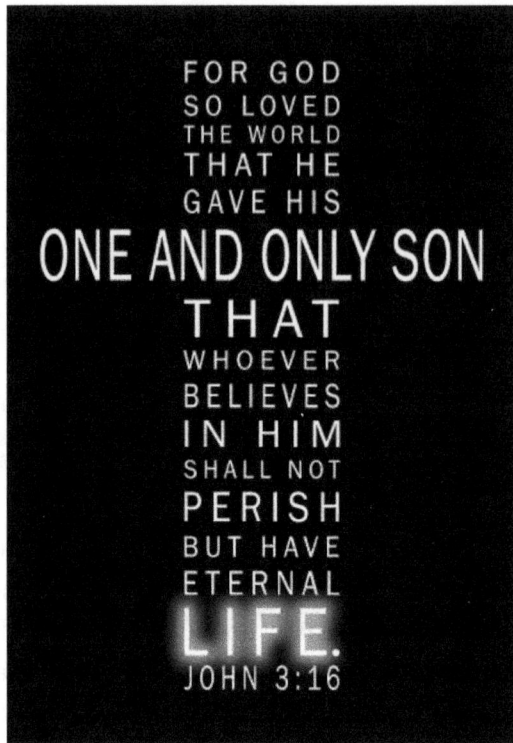

When you look at them like this, God's plan is clear. It begins with *God*. It ends with *Life*. And in between is the *Cross*.

PRAYER

Father, your plan is clear. And it revolves around your Son, whose body—as the bread of communion reminds us—was given for us, and whose blood—like wine or juice—was poured out for us. May we follow Him freely and one day be transformed to live with Him forever. Amen.

MORE TO CONSIDER

Does it not make sense that God would count the cost before creating man? Did you count the cost before becoming a Christian?

---

[1]Max Lucado, *3:16 The Numbers of Hope* (Nashville, TN: Thomas Nelson, Inc, 2007).

14

COMMUNION LITURGIES

W E USE WORDS to convey ideas. And when we use them well, the ideas conveyed—and the very words themselves— are long remembered. The communion liturgies[1] of the Episcopal and Catholic churches are good examples. And many of their words are incorporated in the following thoughts.

It is right, and a good and joyful thing, always and everywhere to give thanks to God, creator of heaven and earth. In His infinite love, He made us for Himself. And when we fell into sin and became subject to evil and death, He in His mercy sent Jesus, His only and eternal Son, to live and die as one of us and to reconcile us to Him.

In Jesus, we see God made visible and are caught up in love of the God we cannot see. In Him, we are delivered from evil and made worthy to stand before God. In Him, we are brought out of error into truth, out of sin into righteousness, out of death into life. On the night that He was handed over to suffering and death, He:

> . . . took bread and when he had given thanks, he broke it and said, "This is my body, which is for you; do this in remembrance of me." In the same way, after supper he took the cup saying, "This cup is the new covenant in my blood; do this, whenever you drink it, in remembrance of me." For whenever you eat this bread and drink this cup, you proclaim the Lord's death until he comes. (1 Cor 11:23-26)

37

So, we eat bread representing His flesh—the body of Christ, the bread of heaven. We drink juice representing His blood—the life of Christ, the cup of salvation.

For on the day following the institution of this meal, He stretched out His arms on a cross and offered Himself—in obedience to God's will—a perfect sacrifice for the whole world. Because God made that sacrifice the sole basis of our salvation, we remember His death, we proclaim His resurrection, we await His coming in glory.

PRAYER

Whether expressed in our own words or in the words of others, we are grateful for Jesus and His sacrifice. "Though you have not seen him, you love him; and though you do not see him now, you believe in him and are filled with an inexpressible and glorious joy" (1 Pet 1:8).

MORE TO CONSIDER

About one-third of U. S. Catholics believe in transubstantiation—the idea that during Mass, the bread and wine become the body and blood of Jesus. They believe that Paul made that clear in his first letter to the Corinthians. Is that how you would interpret Paul's words, or do you see the body and blood as symbols?

---

[1]See, for example, *The Book of Common Prayer* (New York: Church Publishing Incorporated, 1979).

15

DO YOU FEAR GOD?

D O YOU FEAR GOD? Job of the Old Testament certainly did. In the 9th chapter of the book bearing his name, he says this of God:

> If only there were someone to mediate between us, to bring us together, someone to remove God's rod from me, so that his terror would frighten me no more. Then I would speak up without fear of him. (Job 9:33-35)

Job exhibited the kind of fear that churches of past generations were fond of promoting, but that we tend to ignore. We are more likely to quote 1 John 4:18:

> There is no fear in love. But perfect love drives out fear, because fear has to do with punishment. (1 John 4:18)

But the problem is that none of us have perfect love; we all must deal with a little fear. It was appropriate for Jesus to warn us, "Fear him who after the body has been killed, has power to throw you into hell" (Lk 12:5). And for the apostle Paul to caution the Philippians, "continue to work out your salvation with fear and trembling" (Phil 2:12).

The question that arises is this: Can we both fear and love God? And fortunately for us the answer is yes. God's ultimate response to Job's plea for an arbitrator is summarized in 1st Timothy:

> For there is one God and one mediator between God and mankind, the man Christ Jesus, who gave himself as a ransom for all people.
>
> (1 Tim 2:5-6)

Jesus delivered that message on the cross:

- Removing our fear of God's retaliation for our sin.

- Demonstrating the perfect love that John claimed could drive our fear away.

- And becoming the mediator that Job so desperately requested and that we—like Job—so desperately need.

PRAYER

Father, you are to be feared, not to be taken lightly, for we cannot even comprehend your power or your holiness. We are like people standing on the edge of the Grand Canyon, terrified of falling but overwhelmed by your glory and the grace that you offer us through Jesus. He is our mediator in the covenant of grace; His body and blood were sacrificed to establish it. So, we thank you for your Son who relieves our fear. Amen.

MORE TO CONSIDER

Do you fear God? What do fear about Him? Does Jesus reduce your fear?

16

FULFILLING
THE LAW AND THE PROPHETS

IN THE SERMON ON THE MOUNT, Jesus said:

Do not think that I have come to abolish the Law or the Prophets [*that is, the Old Testament*]; I have not come to abolish them, but to fulfill them. (Matt 5:17)

A lot has been written about what Jesus meant when He made that statement. It is easy to read it without giving it enough thought and to simply assume that it means that Jesus fulfilled the Messianic prophecies of the Old Testament. He was born of a virgin, for instance, was a descendent of David, and was betrayed for 30 pieces of silver. Or you might presume that He fulfilled the Law by obeying it perfectly. He lived a life without sin, something that none of us have been able to do.

But there is a less obvious and perhaps more important way that Jesus fulfilled the Law, and it is particularly relevant to our understanding of the Lord's Supper—He fulfilled the *demands of the Law* on each of us. In the Old Testament:

- Death and separation from God were the punishment for everything from murder[1] to kidnapping[2] to working on the Sabbath[3] and even, in some cases, to disobeying your parents.[4]

41

- Thousands of animals were killed annually to atone for the *unintentional* sins of God's people.

So, whether a sin was intentional or unintentional, God made it abundantly clear in the Old Testament that "the wages of sin is death" (Rom 6:23) and separation from Him.

- That is what the Law prescribes for us.

- And that is the demand of the Law that Jesus fulfilled for us.

PRAYER

Father, when Jesus said that He came to fulfill the Law and the Prophets, it was prophetic, because the only way for Him to fulfill the demand of the Law was to one day die and be separated–at least temporarily–from you. That is a sacrificial act that we in no way deserve and can only marvel at and express our gratitude for, as we do just now with the bread and cup of this communion. Amen.

MORE TO CONSIDER

In Matthew 5:21-22, Jesus claims that harboring anger and contempt for someone is as serious as murder. According to Jesus, both make you liable to judgment. Is that an extension of the Old Testament law against murder [i.e., "You shall not murder" (Exod 20:13)] or a redefinition of it?

---

[1]See Leviticus 24:17.

[2]See Exodus 21:16.

[3]See Numbers 15:32-36.

[4]See Deuteronomy 19:6.

THE PASSION OF CHRIST AND CULPABILITY OF MAN

17   A Suffering Servant 45
18   What's Wrong With This Picture? 47
19   Suffering Alone 49
20   Scarred Forever 51
21   Discerning God's Will 55
22   Choices 57
23   The Blood and the Promise 59

THE CRUCIFIXION NARRATIVES describe both the Passion of the Christ and the culpability of man. The Passion, which comes from the Latin word for suffering, was prophesied in the Old Testament. The seven meditations in this section draw from both Testaments and examine what they tell us about Jesus' suffering and man's culpability. The first four meditations are focused on the Passion of Christ. The final three deal with the immediate and ultimate causes of that suffering. The meditations entitled *Isaiah 53* and *My God, My God, Why?* were placed in other sections of the book[1] but also deal with the suffering of Jesus.

---

[1]Meditations 11 and 80, respectively.

17

A SUFFERING SERVANT

THE 22ND AND 69TH PSALMS describe a Godly sufferer from the sufferer's point of view. The writers of the New Testament quoted them more than any of the other Psalms and saw in them the suffering of Christ on the cross. Consider the following verses and imagine the suffering of Jesus for you.

> Dogs have surrounded me. A band of evil men has encircled me. They have pierced my hands and my feet. I can count all my bones. People stare and gloat over me. They divide my garments among them and cast lots for my clothing. (Ps 22:16-18 NIV84)

> Scorn has broken my heart and has left me helpless; I looked for sympathy, but there was none; for comforters but I found none. They put gall in my food and gave me vinegar for my thirst. (Ps 69:20-21)

> I am poured out like water, and all my bones are out of joint. My heart has turned to wax; it has melted away within me. (Ps 22:14)

> My God, my God, why have you forsaken me? Why are you so far from saving me, so far from the words of my groaning? (Ps 22:1)

> Those who hate me without reason outnumber the hairs of my head; many are my enemies without cause, those who seek to destroy me. I am forced to restore what I did not steal. (Ps 69:4)

PRAYER

Our Heavenly Father, we cannot escape the fact that Jesus was forced to restore what we stole. Forgive us for necessitating His suffering. Amen.

MORE TO CONSIDER

Can you imagine the helplessness and hurting suggested by the imagery in these Psalms? Think about what it means to be the creator of all things and subject one's self to the anguish pictured here.

18

WHAT'S WRONG
WITH THIS PICTURE?

NOT SO LONG AGO it was common, when reality did not match perception, to say in a figure of speech, "What's wrong with this picture?" That was a way of saying, "something is not right here." In August 2006, a story with doctored photographs of the Israeli Hezbollah war came out. The Reuters® News Service had distributed several photographs that the photographer had doctored to make the Israelis look bad. The Associated Press was apparently guilty of similar behavior. The motive of the photographer is obvious, but what about the editors who are supposed to catch this sort of thing. The most generous explanation is that they saw what they wanted to see. They wanted Israel to be guilty of excesses, so they asked no questions.

When Jesus instituted the Lord's Supper, He asked us to use it to picture His death so we would not forget it or distort it. On the one hand, we would like to get out our mental Photoshop®, delete the cross, clean up the blood, and put a smile on His face. We do not like thinking about His death, and some churches don't talk about it much.

On the other hand, there is a great sad truth that haunts us. A proper picture of the end of Jesus' stay on earth would have:

- The naked back of every man laid open with whip lashes and His covered with a royal robe.

47

- Every brow pierced with thorns and His covered with a crown.

- Every man pinned bleeding to a cross and Him seated on a spotless white throne.

- Every side punctured with a spear and His untouched.

- Every miserable human being crying out to God with his last breath and Him filled with life.

But even if that picture could be created, it would not change the blessed reality. Thank God, things were not as they should have been at Calvary. We remember with the juice and the bread, the earth's only innocent man lacerated, stabbed, voiceless, breathless, and lifeless. And we ask with wonder, "What's right about this picture?" And we know that nothing is.

Prayer

Our Father, the cost of our salvation was great. We have no real conception of the agony that Jesus endured on the cross or the sadness that you must have felt. But we are grateful for the love that it represents and the life that it makes possible for us in eternity. Amen.

More to Consider

Is your view of the crucifixion distorted? Do you dismiss the suffering of Jesus as easy because He is fully God, or do you think of it as difficult because He was fully man?

19

SUFFERING ALONE

He took my sins and my sorrows,
He made them His very own;
He bore the burden to Calvary,
And suffered, and died alone.

THIS VERSE from the hymn *My Savior's Love*,[1] captures an aspect of the death of Jesus that we sometimes overlook: He suffered and died alone.

- From what began as a triumphal entry and ended with a mob shouting "crucify Him," Jesus suffered and died alone.

- From the disciple who betrayed Him to the one who denied Him and those who scattered at His arrest, Jesus suffered and died alone.

- From the sorrowful prayer in the garden with the disciples a stone's throw away, but sound asleep, Jesus suffered and died alone.

- Saddest of all, from the time they nailed Him to the cross, till He cried out in agony, "My God, My God, why have you forsaken me?" (Mark 15:34), Jesus suffered and died alone.

Our deepest suffering is always alone. Loved ones can gather at the foot of our bed or at the foot of his cross, and they can be in some sense *by* us, but in no sense in our suffering and dying are they *with* us. In today's communion service we are reminded not only that He suffered and died, but that He suffered and died alone. If that were all our communion had to say, we would be of all people most miserable. But:

- Our communion also speaks with the voice of the angel in the garden: "He is not here. He is risen" (Matt 28:6).

- Our communion also speaks with the voice of Mary to the disciples, "He is risen from the dead" (Matt 28:7).

- And more than any other, our communion speaks with the voice of Thomas in the upper room. "My Lord and my God" (John 20:28).

Prayer

Our Father, we regret that Jesus had to do what He did for us alone. We regret that even if we had been there, we would have behaved no differently from the disciples, asleep in the garden, scattered at the arrest. He paid an incalculable price. He achieved an immeasurable victory. The bread and the cup of communion are bittersweet reminders of the cost of His victory until He comes again.

More to Consider

Do you agree with idea that our deepest suffering is always done alone? No one around Jesus could understand what He was going through. That may have been one of the reasons that He frequently sought the solitude of prayer with His Father. Who do you turn to when you are alone in a time of need?

---

[1]Charles H. Gabriel, *My Savior's Love* (Chicago, IL: Hope Publishing Company, 1957), 264.

20

SCARRED FOREVER

J ESUS IS PRAYING in the Garden of Gethsemane just prior to His arrest and crucifixion. He prays three times to God to take away what He calls "this cup." Here is how Luke records it:

"Father, if you are willing, take this cup from me; yet not my will, but yours be done." An angel from heaven appeared to him and strengthened him. And being in anguish, he prayed more earnestly, and his sweat was like drops of blood falling to the ground.

(Luke 22:42-44)

This agonizing prayer was clearly in response to a very serious matter. Something very important was at hand, something that would shake heaven and earth. In a short time, Jesus will suffer and die on the cross. But there is a mistake that we can make when we think about the crucifixion.

We speak so much of His physical suffering that we may be tempted to think that it was this suffering that He dreaded. He would be betrayed by one of His disciples and denied by another. At an unfair trial He would be spit upon, slapped, and struck with fists. He would be whipped, a crown of thorns would be pressed upon His head, and He would be pummeled with a staff—all of this to the point that He was unable to carry His cross. Then, He would be crucified with all the suffering that crucifixion implies. We have often heard described the brutality of crucifixion with the nails

51

in the hands and feet and the cross being lifted in the air and dropped into a waiting hole, the weight of His body on the hands and feet, and the pressure on the lungs that made breathing difficult, but do you know what the Bible says about the crucifixion?

It simply says in three Gospels that "They crucified him." Matthew says, "When they crucified him" (Matt 27:35). That's it. Not one of the details is mentioned. Surprisingly, the word *nail* appears only three times in the New Testament. Thomas won't believe until he sees the nail marks;[1] Paul speaks metaphorically of nailing what he calls our legal indebtedness to the cross;[2] and the most relevant passage is in Peter's sermon on the day of Pentecost, where he speaks of His enemies nailing Him to the cross.[3]

This is not to suggest that we should not remember the physical suffering that He endured. It was excruciating. But the thing He prayed about in the Garden was not a fear of the crucifixion because it was going to hurt. To believe that is to completely misunderstand the Scriptures. It was something else. This verse from 1st Peter captures it well:

> He himself bore our sins in his body on the cross, so that we might die to sins and live for righteousness; by his wounds you have been healed. (1 Pet 2:24)

The thing that Jesus dreaded was this. On the cross He was to bear the sins of the world—all sin past, present, and future. Under that burden, He cried out on the cross, "My God, My God, why have you forsaken me?" (Mark 15:34). For the first time the consequences of sin entered the divine experience, and it would forevermore be a part of who Jesus is. That is why when He was resurrected. He was not raised with a perfect body but with nail scarred hands. The Godhead would be for all eternity scarred by the cost of forgiven sin.

PRAYER

Thank you, our Father, for the cup and the loaf. Their full meaning is beyond our understanding but in as much as we can, we thank you for your love and forgiveness. Amen.

MORE TO CONSIDER

The writers of the New Testament do not describe the crucifixion of Jesus in great detail. The people of that time period were all too familiar with the agony of crucifixion. Have you considered the possibility that bearing the sin of the world was more difficult that the physical agony of crucifixion? What about the idea that God is forever scarred by the crucifixion?

---

[1] See John 20:25.

[2] See Col 2:14.

[3] See Acts 2:23.

21

DISCERNING GOD'S WILL

WHEN RECRUITING Peter and Andrew to be among his first disciples, Jesus said *follow me.* "Come, follow me, and I will send you out to fish for people" (Matt 4:19). When a rich young ruler wanted to know what it would take for him to inherit eternal life, Jesus said "sell everything you have and give to the poor... Then come, follow me" (Mark 10:21). And when sending out the apostles to proclaim that the kingdom of heaven was near, Jesus said "Whoever does not take up their cross and follow me is not worthy of me" (Matt 10:38). Time after time, Jesus asked people to follow Him, because He knew that it was God's will that they do so.

But when people, exercising their God-given free will, failed to follow Jesus, when they instead betrayed Him and sought to kill Him, Jesus found Himself in a difficult position. In the Garden of Gethsemane, on the eve of His crucifixion, thinking about God's will for His life, He must have asked Himself, 'Is it really God's will for me to die at the hands of men who were created to follow me?" He prayed, 'Father, if you are willing, take this cup from me; yet not my will, but yours be done" (Luke 22:42). And He made peace with the fact that:

- It was "the Lord's will to crush him and cause him to suffer" (Isa 53:10), as Isaiah had prophesied.

- And that His suffering would be the means by which God would accomplish His ultimate will—that we follow Jesus of our own free will.

How many of us would follow Him if he had merely performed a few miracles long ago and demonstrated a keen understanding of scripture? We follow Jesus because of the cross. Forgiveness, reconciliation with God, and the gift of the Holy Spirit were made possible on the cross. And we use the bread and cup of communion to remember the cross. And because we want to follow the one who gave Himself upon it.

PRAYER

Father, we know that it is your will for us to follow your Son. And what better reason could we have than the cross, than His sacrifice, than forgiveness and reconciliation and eternal life with you? Help us—relying on the Holy Spirit—to follow the one who died for us and in whose name we pray. Amen.

MORE TO CONSIDER

Do you think that it was easy for Jesus to know God's will for His life? Is it easy for you? Would you have interpreted Isaiah's prophecy in the same way that Jesus evidently did?

22

CHOICES

This is my body, given for you, do this in remembrance of me... This cup is the new covenant in my blood, which is poured out for you.
(Luke 22:19, 20)

THOSE ARE THE WORDS OF JESUS as recorded in the 22nd chapter of Luke. He said them to the apostles in the upper room on the day before He was killed. Rather than leave Jerusalem and avoid the suffering that He had been predicting for almost a year, Jesus told the apostles to remember His body, as if it had already been broken, and to remember His blood, as if it had already been shed. In both requests, He included the words "for you"—my body, given for you; my blood, poured out for you. We don't know what the apostles understood Jesus to mean when He made those requests, but one thing that was surely implied is this—I am choosing to die for you.

The choices made over the next 24 hours were not so admirable:

- Judas chose to betray him.

- Peter chose to deny him.

- Herod chose to ignore him.

And in the end, when the crowd had gathered, according to Matthew 27, Pilate asked them all,

> "Which one do you want me to release to you: Jesus Barabbas, or Jesus who is called the Messiah?" For he knew it was out of self-interest that they had handed Jesus over to him.   (Matt 27:17-18)

> "Which of the two do you want me to release to you?" asked the governor. "Barabbas," they answered. "What shall I do, then, with Jesus who is called the Messiah?" Pilate asked.   (Matt 27:21–22)

They all answered, *we all answered,* "Crucify him!" The Son of God became a man and chose to die for you.

PRAYER

We are grateful for the choice that Jesus made, and we ask your forgiveness for all the sinful choices that we have made. Amen.

MORE TO CONSIDER

How are the choices made by Judas, Pilate, and Herod like the choices that people make today about Jesus? The series of choices described here are the immediate cause of and resulted in Jesus' crucifixion. What was the ultimate cause?

23

THE BLOOD AND THE PROMISE

"What shall I do, then, with Jesus who is called the Messiah?" Pilate asked. They all answered, "Crucify him!" ... "I am innocent of this man's blood," he said. "It is your responsibility!" All the people answered, "Let his blood be on us and on our children!"   (Matt 27:22-25)

"Therefore let all Israel be assured of this: God has made this Jesus, whom you crucified, both Lord and Messiah." When the people heard this, they were cut to the heart and said to Peter and the other apostles, "Brothers, what shall we do?" Peter replied, "Repent and be baptized, every one of you, in the name of Jesus Christ for the forgiveness of your sins. And you will receive the gift of the Holy Spirit. The promise is for you and your children and for all who are far off—for all whom the Lord our God will call."   (Acts 2:36-39)

CONSIDER THESE TWO PASSAGES, "All the people answered, 'Let his blood be on us and on our children!'" (Matt 27:25) and 'The promise is for you and your children!' (Acts 2:39).

When Mel Gibson made *The Passion of The Christ*,[1] he had to remove the 'Let his blood be on us and on our children" from the film[2] because it offended those who make a living being offended. If he had produced a movie on The Sermon of Peter, he would have had to cut a good bit of it out, too. What the professional victims do not understand is that the Jews represented all of us in their response to Christ. If we had been there, we would have done what they did. We each in our own way have done what they did. We have rejected Christ. What is described in Matthew 27 is not the response of Jews to a Jew or even humans to a human. It is the response of humanity to God. In an otherwise awkward interview with Diane Sawyer, Mel Gibson said the most profound thing that will likely ever fall from his lips. Asked who killed Jesus, he said, "We all did."[3] Whether planned or spontaneous, he performed what may be his most meaningful part he will ever play, when in the filming of the movie, he grabbed the hammer from another's hand and drove the nail into Jesus' hand himself. We all killed Jesus—those of us who have sinned.

The death of Jesus divided humanity into two groups, those rebels and their children who reject God and crucify His son by their rejection ("Let his blood be on us and on our children") and those who accept the death of Christ as atonement for their sins, of whom the Scripture says, "The promise is for you and your children."

It is the promise we celebrate. It is with hope that all people everywhere will come to forgiveness through the death of Christ. It is with sadness that our sins have been so destructive. It is with thankfulness that He paid so great a price to set us free.

PRAYER

Lord, bless the cup as it represents the blood of Christ shed from His thorn-stuck brow, His whip-gashed back, His nail-stabbed hands and feet, and His spear-lanced side, all for the sin of the world and for our sin in particular. Bless the loaf as it represents His stretched and twisted flesh, tense with pain, caked with blood, parched in the sun, freely given for us. May we never forget. Amen.

MORE TO CONSIDER

Did you notice the phrases "and our children" and "and your children" in the passages under consideration? If you have chosen to receive the *promise*, what have you done to ensure that your children do as well?

---

[1] *The Passion of the Christ*, directed by Mel Gibson (Newmarket Films, 2004).

[2] Sharon Waxman, 'Gibson To Delete A Scene in 'Passion,'" The New York Times, February 4, 2004, https://www.nytimes.com/2004/02/04/movies/gibson-to-delete-a-scene-in-passion.html.

[3] Diane Sawyer, 'Diane Sawyer Interviews Mel Gibson – The Passion of the Christ Special" ABC News, January 4, 2016, 42:39, https://m.youtube.com/watch?v=096Bx3dtjNo.

THE PURPOSE
OF THE LORD'S SUPPER

24	Becoming More Like Jesus	65
25	Examining Our Expectations	67
26	Reinforcing Our Beliefs	71
27	Remembering God's Promises	73
28	The Second Communion	75
29	Celebrating the Death of Jesus	77
30	Remembering the Agony of the Cross	79
31	Proclaiming the Lord's Death	81
32	How to Remember	83
33	Finding the Right Perspective	85
34	Remembering God's Presence	87
35	The Supremacy of Jesus	89
36	Drawing Close to Christ	91
37	Remembering Essential Truths	93
38	A Room Called Remember Him	95
39	The Greatness of Jesus	97

ACCORDING TO JESUS HIMSELF, the overarching purpose of the Lord's Supper is to memorialize Him and His death. In Luke's account of the institution of the Lord's Supper, Jesus states it directly: "Do this in remembrance of me" (Luke 22:19). Thus, many of the meditations in this section are devoted to that end (and have titles like *Remembering God's Promises, Remembering God's Presence, ...*). Communion, however, fulfills several other important functions in the life of a Christian, including reinforcing beliefs, reminding us of God's presence and promises, and so on. And these are considered in the essays of this section as well. Additionally, many of the meditations in the section entitled *The Bread and Cup as Symbols*—like *Ordinary Symbols of Extraordinary Meaning*[1]—could have been placed here as well.

[1]Meditations 40.

24

BECOMING MORE LIKE JESUS

IN 1ST CORINTHIANS 11, the apostle Paul wrote that when the Christians at Corinth took the Lord's Supper in an unworthy manner, they became "weak and sick," and some even died. He believed that communion, taken irreverently, had adverse physical consequences. That is hard for us to imagine, because our physical health does not seem to be linked to communion. But it raises an interesting question: Does the Lord's Supper have any effect, positive or negative, on our lives?

Many widely read and highly regarded authors believe that it does. In the book *Mere Christianity*, for example, C. S. Lewis wrote:[1]

> There are three things that spread the Christ-life to us: baptism, belief, and that mysterious action which different Christians call by different names—Holy Communion, the Mass, the Lord's Supper.

He saw communion as something that God uses to change us into what he called "little Christs."

Theologian N. T. Wright offers a practical explanation for all the changes that take place in the hearts and minds of Christians, including those associated with the practice of communion. He asserts:[2]

> You become like what you worship. When you gaze in awe, admiration, and wonder at something or someone, you begin to take on ... the character of the object of your worship.

65

Since communion is at the heart of our worship, it makes sense that:

- When we reflect reverently on the meaning of the words "This is my body given for you ... This cup is the new covenant in my blood, which is poured out for you"

- When we take the bread and cup in admiration of the one who spoke them

- When amazed by His selflessness, we judge ourselves by the standard He set, so that as Paul told the Corinthians, we will not later come under judgment

- When we do those things with regularity

God can change us. And we become a little more like what we worship—a little more kind and caring, a little more selfless, a little more obedient, a little more like Jesus, whose life, death, and resurrection make the change in us possible.

PRAYER

Father, use this time around your table to change us. Like Paul, "we want to know Christ and the power of his resurrection and the fellowship of sharing in his sufferings, becoming like him in his death, and so, somehow, to attain the resurrection from the dead" (Phil 3:10). We thank you again for Jesus and pray this in His name. Amen.

MORE TO CONSIDER

Do you think that communion has affected you in a positive way? What effect has it had? Does it make sense to think of those effects as a part of the purpose of the Lord's Supper?

---

[1]C. S. Lewis, *Mere Christianity* (New York: Simon & Schuster, 1996), 63.

[2]N. T. Wright, *Simply Christian* (New York: HarperCollins, 2006), 148.

25

EXAMINING
OUR EXPECTATIONS

So they prepared the Passover. When evening came, Jesus arrived with the Twelve. While they were reclining at the table eating, he said, "Truly I tell you, one of you will betray me—one who is eating with me." They were saddened, and one by one they said to him, "Surely you don't mean me?" "It is one of the Twelve," he replied, "one who dips bread into the bowl with me. The Son of Man will go just as it is written about him. But woe to that man who betrays the Son of Man! It would be better for him if he had not been born."

While they were eating, Jesus took bread, and when he had given thanks, he broke it and gave it to his disciples, saying, "Take it; this is my body." Then he took a cup, and when he had given thanks, he gave it to them, and they all drank from it. "This is my blood of the covenant, which is poured out for many," he said to them. "Truly I tell you, I will not drink again from the fruit of the vine until that day when I drink it new in the kingdom of God."

When they had sung a hymn, they went out to the Mount of Olives. (Mark 14:16-26)

THE LORD'S SUPPER was instituted at a Passover Celebration during which the Jews remembered their Exodus from Egypt. They did so annually. And when Jesus celebrated His last

67

Passover with the apostles, most Jews were hoping for a similar release from their bondage under the Roman empire. But more was happening in the Upper Room and on the cross that followed the next day than can be explained by these facts alone. More was happening than can be explained by all the communion meditations in all the churches in all the world over all of time.

N. T. Wright identifies seven important themes in the Exodus and associated Passover celebration:

1. A wicked tyrant—Pharaoh.

2. A chosen leader—Moses.

3. A victory by God—the plagues and the Red Sea drowning of Pharaoh's armies.

4. A rescue by sacrifice—which is specifically what Passover celebrated, sacrificing a lamb and spreading his blood on the door frame.

5. A new calling and way of life—the Ten Commandments.

6. The presence of God—leading them with a pillar of cloud by day and fire by night.

7. And the promised Land—fulfillment of the promise made to Abraham, Isaac, and Jacob.

And they are not just themes, but the essence of the worldview of first century Jews. They were ingrained in their thinking. Oppressed Jews were expecting something like the Exodus to happen again, and when Jesus comes:

1. He overcomes a wicked tyrant—not the Jewish leaders, not even Rome as the Jews hoped, but rather Satan himself.

2. He is God's Chosen leader, the Messiah. But He does not lead the kind of army He is expected to lead. He announces that God is now King.

3. He demonstrates God's victory by healing, by forgiveness, and by celebrating.

4. He rescues people by means of a sacrifice. He is that sacrifice.

5. He calls people to a new way of life, the way of going the second mile, turning the other cheek, loving enemies, and praying for them, even as He did on the cross.

6. He is the presence of God Immanuel, God with us. He is the fulfillment of all the hopes and promises of Israel.

7. And finally, He leads his people to the Promised Land—a new kingdom with a new kind of king where they will experience abundant life that begins in this reality and extends for eternity. He was not what people expected, but He was everything that the Exodus promised.

Some rejected Him because they rejected the kind of Kingdom He represented or they were afraid, but to those who accepted Him He gave the power to become children of God. That is a lot to think about during communion, but it is only a little of what the Lord's Supper and death of Jesus is all about.

PRAYER

Lord, we know we are not saved by our understanding, but we are enriched by it. We cannot comprehend all the expectations the Jews had for the coming king, nor can we understand the ways Jesus was misunderstood and mistreated. But we know what He did and what He did for our salvation, and we thank you for it. We worship you as we remember His body with the bread and His blood with the cup and as we pray in His name. Amen.

MORE TO CONSIDER

The expectations of the Jewish leaders of Jesus' day were way off the mark. Is it possible that some of our own expectations are not completely without fault? What expectations do you bring to the table of remembrance?

26

REINFORCING OUR BELIEFS

I N THE BOOK *Mere Christianity,*[1] C. S. Lewis confesses that when he was an atheist, there were times when Christianity looked highly probable. And that after becoming a Christian, there were times when the whole thing seemed highly improbable. He concluded that:

- You cannot be a sound atheist or a sound Christian without learning to control your moods.

- And beliefs do not just automatically stay alive in our minds. We must be continually reminded of what we believe.

If that is the case, if frequent exposure to ideas, once accepted, is the key to holding on to them, then communion is one of our most important faith-building exercises. For of all the things we do in church, it alone always focuses attention on that which is central to the Christian faith. There are many reasons to worship God, people pray for all sorts of things, and the Bible reveals countless truths. But communion is always about "Christ and him crucified" (1 Cor 2:2).

When the bread and the cup are passed to you, and you turn to God in prayer, and you recall that Jesus' body was broken like the bread in your hands, and His blood was poured out like the juice in your cup, and that—just as He explained to the apostles in the upper room—it was all

71

done "for you" (Luke 22:19-20), then exactly like Jesus intended, you are reminded of the one thing you must hold on to regardless of your mood— His atoning death on the cross.

PRAYER

We are grateful that through the bread and the cup and what they represent, we see the extent of your unfailing love for us. As we reflect upon that love and the forgiveness we are extended because of it, may our belief in the redeeming power of your Son's death become even stronger. Amen.

MORE TO CONSIDER

Have you ever found yourself questioning a belief because you had forgotten why you believed it in the first place? Does your participation in the Lord's Supper reinforce your belief in Jesus and His death and resurrection?

---

[1]C. S. Lewis, *Mere Christianity* (New York: Simon & Schuster, 1996), 125.

27

REMEMBERING GOD'S PROMISES

IN THE EARLY DAYS of humanity, people became so evil that God destroyed them with a great flood, saving only Noah and his family. One can imagine the instability of subsequent generations and their fear of rain. They might have said, "Is this the way it is going to be? Every time God becomes unhappy with us, He will destroy us with a flood." In order to bring stability to the earth, God promised them that He would never again destroy the earth with a flood and assured His people of this truth by giving them a sign—the rainbow. He says in effect that the rainbow will remind Him of His promise to them. And it would certainly remind them of that promise. No matter how hard the rain, how severe the thunder, how bright the lightning, God's people had His promise. The storm would end.

There was a similar instability during the upheaval associated with the betrayal and crucifixion of Jesus. The world of his followers was destroyed. One might imagine His Apostles saying, "Is this the way it is going to be? He comes among us and teaches us the word of God and they kill Him. In time He may be forgotten." God also provided them with a sign, a reminder of His promise. Paul describes it in 1 Corinthians 11:23-25:

> For I received from the Lord what I also passed on to you: The Lord Jesus, on the night he was betrayed, took bread, and when he had given thanks, he broke it and said, "This is my body, which is for you;

> do this in remembrance of me." In the same way, after supper he took the cup, saying, "This cup is the new covenant in my blood; do this, whenever you drink it, in remembrance of me."   (1 Cor 11:23-25)

Then Paul says, "For whenever you eat this bread and drink this cup, you proclaim the Lord's death until he comes" (1 Cor 11:26).

In the presence of persecution and all the uncertainties of the first century world, where people lost their jobs, their homes, and their families because of their faith, the Lord's Supper was the symbol of something that was certain and unchanging. Four of the things that were certain and unchanging were that:

1. Jesus loved them enough to die for them.
2. God raised Him from the dead.
3. He would be present with them through His spirit.
4. He was coming again to take them with Him.

Our lives too are characterized by change. Not many things seem certain. That is why we must place our greatest trust in the things that do not change. Just as Israel saw the rainbow and was reminded of God's promise, we see the communion and are reminded of the power, love, and the faithfulness of God. These are things that will not change no matter what else does. All our lives are rocked and shocked by change. At the communion table we celebrate eternal certainties.

PRAYER

Father, we are grateful for the confidence we have through Jesus. We know that He loves us, is present with us in spirit, and is coming again to take us to be with Him. Amen.

MORE TO CONSIDER

Think about the uncertainties that you face in life. What are the things that you most count on and take comfort from when change seems to be overwhelming? Is Jesus one of them?

THE PURPOSE OF THE LORD'S SUPPER

28

THE SECOND COMMUNION

IT WAS SUPPOSED to be an ordinary Passover meal, but when Jesus said, "I have eagerly desired to eat this Passover with you," and then added "before I suffer" (Luke 22:14), the apostles should have known that it was going to be anything but ordinary. When He gave them bread and wine and said, "This is my body, given for you... This cup is the new covenant in my blood, which is poured out for you" (Luke 22:19), the word "new" and the fact that the old covenant was sealed by the shedding of blood, should have put them all on high alert. Things were about to change.

But as the apostles held the bread and cup of the very first communion service in their hands—with the yet-to-be-sacrificed body and blood of Jesus present—they could not comprehend what those emblems would one day mean. Over the next few days, they would struggle with the fact that Jesus had died; over the next few years, they would come to understand the meaning and theology of His death.

We do not know when or where the second communion service took place. But it is hard not to imagine that those same apostles—minus Judas Iscariot—were present, and that their frame of mind was radically different.

- For when they next distributed the bread and recalled the phrase, "my body, given for you," surely they pictured Jesus' lifeless body hanging on a cross.

- When they drank the wine, knowing that it represented His poured-out blood, how could they not imagine the nails in His hands... His spear-lanced side?

- And when they began to piece together the new covenant ideas of redemption, atonement, grace, and reconciliation, surely Jesus' resurrection from the dead bolstered their confidence in all those things.

Only after the apostles had encountered the resurrected Jesus could they truly understand what we understood the very first time we came to the Lord's Table: That the *breaking of bread* is the appointed way of remembering Jesus—that He died for our sins, made forgiveness possible, and set things right between God and us.

PRAYER

Our heavenly Father, may we commune together this morning with the same confidence that the apostles had after witnessing the resurrection and coming to understand why Jesus had to die and what His death accomplished for each of us. Thank you for Jesus and it is in His name that we pray. Amen.

MORE TO CONSIDER

It is hard to imagine the change of perspective that the apostles must have undergone between their first and second communions. If you have participated in multiple communion services yourself, has your perspective on the meaning of the bread and cup changed over time?

29

CELEBRATING THE DEATH OF JESUS

C ONSIDERING ALL the things Jesus said and did, does it surprise you that the thing He asked us to remember in a special way is His death. Why do you suppose that is?

- He could have asked us to exchange gifts in celebration of His birth every year, saying 'Do this in remembrance of my incarnation." We do that anyway, but He did not ask us to do it.

- He could have asked us to come together once a week and quote an important passage of Scripture, ensuring that we would never forget it. The greatest commandment—that we love God first and our neighbor as ourselves—would be a good one. He could have said, 'Do this in remembrance of my revelation."

- He could have asked us to celebrate His miracles through a healing service every Sunday. He might have said, 'Do this in remembrance of my compassion."

- Or how about celebrating the resurrection. What is more important than that? When the apostles were looking for someone to replace Judas, it had to be someone who had witnessed the resurrection. In the first Gospel sermon, Peter proclaimed, 'God raised Jesus," and to this day, that is the heart of the Good News. Paul said that without the resurrection, our faith is in vain. And the reason we meet on the first day of the week is because it is the day of the resurrection.

But Christ does not call on us to in some symbolic way reenact any of these things. No. What He asked us to do was to remember His death. That is the thing that we might forget in the excitement of our new life. Think of our annual celebration of the Holy Week. We celebrate Good Friday, and we must be careful to remind ourselves why we celebrate it. Really, we only pause on Good Friday in our rush to Resurrection Sunday. Unlike the early followers of Jesus, we know where the story is going. They did not. They suffered heartbreak and grief. It was real to them, and it was a sad memory as long as they lived. We, on the other hand, will not forget His birth, or His life and teaching. However, bathing in the glory of His living presence, without the institution of the Lord's Supper, we might forget the cost of our salvation, so we do this to remember His death.

PRAYER

Father, with the bread and the juice, we remember Christ's suffering and bleeding for us. Before He overcame death, He died. In most of what we do as a church we celebrate His resurrection, but just now with deep gratitude, we remember and celebrate His death. Amen.

MORE TO CONSIDER

Have you attended funerals in which you celebrated someone's death? Do you consider the Lord's Supper to be a celebration of Jesus's death? If so, what exactly is there to celebrate?

30

REMEMBERING THE AGONY OF THE CROSS

W E HAVE PHONES that take pictures, so we take pictures of nearly everything, especially ourselves. When we are not taking selfies, security cameras are capturing our every move. Besides that, at every attraction we attend, someone wants to take our picture and give it to us for a price. Sometimes we hire people to take pictures at events like graduations and weddings. But there is one place that we do not seem to take pictures—at funerals. Families come together that have not seen each other for years, but we do not generally take a lot of pictures. We might show pictures of the highlights of the deceased person's life, but we do not take pictures of the funeral like we do at weddings.

Normally, suffering and death are not things to be remembered. We do not want to remember our loved one's suffering. We remind ourselves that their suffering is over. We do not want to think about them lying still in the casket; we want to remember them vibrant and active. We usually do not want to remember what they accomplished in their deaths, but rather what they accomplished in their lives. Sometimes a person achieves a specific good by his death, as when a good man dies saving another life, but generally speaking death is not the topic, even at funerals.

But the death of Jesus is different. He not only instructs us to remember Him, but to remember His death. His pierced flesh and His shed blood are at the center of our remembrance. He gives us more than a picture. We participate in a ceremony of remembrance by eating and drinking, and it is not a feast that we eat like at a thanksgiving dinner, where we can easily remember what the meal was but can forget what the meal was about. But this meal is a tiny piece of bread and a taste of the fruit of the vine, so that the focus of our attention can be on the meaning more than the meal.

We give all this attention to His death, because His death is different from any other. His death accomplished something eternal. What He accomplished was in a sense for the general good of mankind, but more specifically for those who wear His name and gather to remember Him by means of what we call the loaf and the cup. His death made every other death bearable, because it took away the victory of death. While it would be strange indeed for us to celebrate the deaths of others with emphasis on their agony and suffering and bleeding, those are the very things we remember about Him this morning, and because He did it for us, we remember with thanksgiving and praise.

> **And as they were eating, Jesus took bread, and gave thanks, and broke it, and gave it to the disciples, and said, "Take, eat; this is my body." Then he took the cup, and gave thanks, and gave it to them, saying, "Drink from it, all of you. This is my blood of the New Covenant, which is poured out for many for the forgiveness of sins."** (Matt 26:26-28)

PRAYER

Thank you, Lord, for reminding us every week of your death, for in the sacrifice of your body we find hope and in the shedding of your blood we find life. By participating in the Lord's Supper, we remember what you did for us and we proclaim you to the world as our dead and risen Savior. Amen.

MORE TO CONSIDER

Have you ever taken a picture of a loved one that has died? Do you try to remember their death? What makes the death of Jesus worth remembering?

31

Proclaiming
The Lord's Death

Y OU CAN look at the world around you and seeing its beauty and complexity and usefulness to humanity, conclude that it did not come about by chance—that God designed it for man. You can look inside yourself and hear a voice urging you to do right and making you feel responsible and uncomfortable when you do wrong,[1] and conclude that God wants you to be a better person than you now are. But you cannot look at the universe—or even into your own soul—and discover that Jesus died on a cross so that you can become the better person He wants you to be. God expects us to learn that through the writings of the apostles, to remember it through the practice of communion, and to bear witness to it through our remembering.

When Moses was explaining the importance of the Passover meal before leading the Exodus from Egypt, he said to the Israelites:

> And when your children ask you, "What does this ceremony mean to you?" then tell them, "It is the Passover sacrifice to the Lord, who passed over the houses of the Israelites in Egypt and spared our homes when he struck down the Egyptians." (Exod 12:26-27)

It is not an accident that when Jesus met with the apostles in the upper room, He gave new meaning to the bread and wine of the traditional Passover meal and said to start using them to remember Him. So, when our children ask us "What does this ceremony mean to you?" we can similarly say: It is to remember the sacrifice of Jesus, whose suffering and death make it possible for the Lord to pass over our sin and spare our lives when He strikes down those who do not trust in Him. You see, it is just as the apostle Paul once noted, the very act of remembering sends a message to everyone around us:

> "For whenever you eat this bread and drink this cup, you proclaim the Lord's death until he comes." (1 Cor 11:26)

PRAYER

Because we learn about the atoning death of Jesus in the same way that we learn about most historical events, we are grateful for your written Word and for those who have passed it down to us. May we be as diligent in passing it on to others? And now, may we glorify your Son as we proclaim His death through our remembering this morning. Amen.

MORE TO CONSIDER

Have you ever considered the Lord's Supper to be a witness to those around you? If you have children, has it given you the opportunity to explain what the death of Jesus is all about?

---

[1]C. S. Lewis, *Mere Christianity* (New York: Simon & Schuster, 1996), 34.

32

HOW TO REMEMBER

ACCORDING TO LUKE, Jesus "took bread, gave thanks and broke it, and gave it to them, saying, 'This is my body given for you; do this in remembrance of me.' In the same way, after the supper he took the cup, saying, 'This cup is the new covenant in my blood, which is poured out for you'" (Luke 22:19-20). That moment is among the Bible's most remembered:

- It is one of the few that we talk about weekly.

- It is the subject of a world-famous painting—*The Last Supper* by Leonardo Da Vinci.

- And it defines communion as Jesus intended it to be.

He taught us how to remember in the upper room. But:

- It was not there that "God made him who had no sin to be sin for us" (2 Cor 5:21).

- It was not in the upper room that Jesus "redeemed us from the curse of the law by becoming a curse for us" (Gal 3:13).

- And it was not the upper room that Jesus was thinking about when He instituted the Lord's Supper.

He asked the apostles to remember the events of the next day:

- At the place where His body would be tortured and broken.

- Where He would be separated from God and cry out "My God, my God, why have you forsaken me?" (Matt 27:46).

- Where He would be treated as though He were our sin—accepting the role of sin as God unleashed His wrath against it.

- And where we would find out not only how much God hates sin, but how much He loves us.

Remember that this morning—for we do not come to the Lord's Table to remember the institution of the Lord's Supper, but to remember the Lord Himself.

PRAYER

As we share the bread and the cup this morning, help us to see beyond the moment that Jesus shared them with the apostles to the moment that He became them for us—so that we can appreciate the miraculous exchange that took place on the cross, where Jesus became our sin and made it possible for us to become His righteousness. Amen.

MORE TO CONSIDER

Does thinking about the circumstances surrounding the institution of the Lord's Supper ever prevent you from focusing on the one who instituted it?

33

FINDING THE RIGHT PERSPECTIVE

I N 2004, a movie[1] was released in which a man falls in love with a woman who has a serious memory problem. To Henry's dismay, Lucy cannot remember him from one day to the next. Every night, while she is asleep, her memory of the previous day—and of Henry—is erased. So, to get around the problem, Henry creates a special home movie for Lucy to watch every morning. And in it, he reminds her of these three things: (1) who he is, (2) what her problem is, and (3) what their relationship is. Because we sometimes forget God as easily as Lucy forgot Henry, communion functions for us a lot like Henry's movie did for Lucy:

1. We come to this table to remember the one who instituted it—the nails in His hands, His bleeding brow, the frailty of His broken body. Odd things to remember about the maker of all things. But Jesus' purposeful death on the cross tells us more about God and His Son than anything short of heaven ever will.

2. We come to this table and remember our problem—our sin—and not just the indiscretions of youth or the poor decisions made before becoming a Christian. Paul said, "All have sinned and fall short" (Rom 3:23). But our experience is that falling short is a

never-ending problem. And the forgiveness made possible by Jesus' death is an ongoing need.

3.   And we come to this table to remember our relationship with God. Jesus called it a covenant—the "new covenant" (Luke 22:20). The writer of Hebrews called Jesus its "mediator" (Heb 9:15). And in the only recorded use of the term prior to Jesus' use in the upper room, Jeremiah wrote:

> "The time is coming," declares the LORD, "when I will make a new covenant with the people of Israel and with the people of Judah. . ."
>
> "This is the covenant I will make. . . I will put my law in their minds and write it on their hearts. I will be their God, and they will be my people. . ."
>
> "For I will forgive their wickedness and will remember their sins no more."   (Jer 31:31-34)

Living in a good world gone bad, it is not always easy or convenient to remember these things. So, we come to this table to further instill them in our hearts and minds.

PRAYER

Help us to remember. To remember Jesus—your Son and our Savior. To remember our problem—our sin. And to remember our covenant relationship with you. Amen.

MORE TO CONSIDER

There are many things that can be remembered when participating in the Lord's Supper, but are any of them more important than who Jesus is, what our problem is, and what our relationship with God is supposed to be?

---

[1]*Fifty First Dates.* Directed by Peter Segal (2004; Columbia Pictures).

34

REMEMBERING GOD'S PRESENCE

OCIOLOGIST AND MARKET RESEARCHER George Barna has studied the religious beliefs and behavior of Americans for more than two decades. And in an interview about the growing number of Americans who do not go to church, he noted that when churchless people visit a church, they are not looking for the hottest guitarist in town, or the greatest light show, or even the best speaker behind the microphone. What they want to experience, but do not, is the presence of God. Something that we all want and need and that every Christian is promised.[1]

It is a promise that goes all the way back to the time of Abraham. Moses conveyed it to the Israelites when he wrote: "...the Lord your God goes with you; he will never leave you nor forsake you" (Deut 31:6). And over a thousand years later, Jesus—being one with the Father—restated it like this: "And surely I am with you always, to the very end of the age" (Matt 28:20). And then, before returning to the Father, He promised an "Advocate"—the Holy Spirit—who He said would "be with you forever" (John 14:16).

God is with us at this very moment. And one of the purposes of communion is to remind us of His presence. Jesus likened the bread and cup of communion to His own body and blood.[2] And does not a body denote a presence and blood denote life? As much as He wanted us to remember the price paid for our redemption, He also wanted us to remember that He is alive and present with us.

So, think about His presence this morning, as evidenced by your own relationship with Him—for communion presumes that a covenant relationship already exists. Reflect upon all that He has done in your life to bring you to this moment of communion—for His presence is often best recognized in retrospect. And do not fixate on "feeling" His presence—because a feeling, though nice, is not what was promised. As the apostle Paul told the Romans, "The righteous will live by faith" (Rom 1:17).

PRAYER

Father, we thank you that Jesus was once physically present on this earth and that He sacrificed His body and blood to atone for our sin. We thank you that He is with us today. And we pray that the way in which we live our lives will help others see that He is alive and present and active in the world today. Amen.

MORE TO CONSIDER

Is the Lord's Supper an emotional experience for you? Do you think that it should or has to be? How do you know that you are in the presence of God or that God is with you?

---

[1]"George Barna & David Kinnaman on the Rise of the Churchless," Barna.com, January 8, 2015, https://www.barna.org/barna-update/culture/702-george-barna-david-kinnaman-on-the-rise-of-the-churchless.

[2]See Matt 26:26-28

35

THE SUPREMACY OF JESUS

And he is the head of the body, the church: he is the beginning and the firstborn from among the dead, so that in everything he might have the supremacy. For God was pleased to have all his fullness dwell in him, and through him to reconcile to himself all things, whether things on earth or things in heaven, by making peace through his blood, shed on the cross.   (Col 1:18-20)

JESUS SAID of the Lord's Supper, 'Do this... in remembrance of me" (1 Cor 11:25). Paul also wrote, 'For whenever you eat this bread and drink this cup, you proclaim the Lord's death..." (1 Cor 11:26). We observe the Lord's Supper weekly, as we believe was the practice of the early church, and almost always emphasize the Lord's death. However, it is worth noting that one cannot separate out the defining experiences in the Lord's life as though they could stand alone.

In His birth, He was God become flesh. We celebrate that on Christmas. He was, as the ancient confessions say, fully God and fully man. They called Him Jesus (that was His name). They called him Christ (that was His title meaning anointed). He lived a perfect life, taught as no man taught, healed the sick, cast out demons, and performed other miracles.

He came to seek and to save the lost. But He threatened the religious and political powers of His time, and they executed Him. We remember that on Good Friday. In His death, He substituted himself for us and bore our sins, so that we could receive the promise of God.

Three days later He rose from the dead. We celebrate that on Easter. His resurrection proved that He was who He said He was, that all He taught and promised was true, including the reality of the forgiveness of our sins.

Forty days after His resurrection, after showing Himself to His followers, on one occasion to 500 of them, He ascended into heaven in the sight of His disciples whom He commissioned to take His good news into all the world. We do not celebrate the ascension like Easter and Christmas, but it is important, because it tells us where He is today. As Paul says, "Christ Jesus who died—more than that, who was raised to life—is at the right hand of God and is also interceding for us" (Rom 8:34).

Furthermore, His ascension positions Him for the next great event in human history—His coming again. An event to which Paul refers to when he says, "For whenever you eat this bread and drink this cup, you proclaim the Lord's death until he comes" (1 Cor 11:26). In that day, heaven and earth will celebrate as every knee bows and every tongue confesses that He is Lord of all.

So as you participate in the Lord's Supper, remember Jesus, remember the Christ. The Bible is all about Jesus. The Church is all about Jesus. The creation is all about Jesus. Life is all about Jesus. And when we are at our best, we are all about Jesus, the anointed one of God.

PRAYER

Our Father, it is easy to forget the scope of your plan to bring everything under the supremacy of Jesus, who is in fact the source of and purpose for everything. Thank you for reminding us of this in the Lord's Supper. Amen.

MORE TO CONSIDER

In what way does the Lord's Supper remind you of the supremacy of Jesus?

36

DRAWING
CLOSE TO CHRIST

IN OCTOBER OF 2000, a story appeared about a tiny fragment of Christ's cross that was stolen from the base of a statue in St. Michael's Cathedral in Toronto, Canada.

You may wonder how a piece of Christ's cross survived to be in Toronto. The story is that Helena, the mother of Emperor Constantine, went on a pilgrimage in the year 326 and visited the places Jesus had walked. She believed she had identified every site from Jesus's life. She is said to have found the tomb of Jesus and in it three crosses. She brought a dying woman to the scene and had her lie on each cross. The one that healed her she determined to be the cross of Jesus. Relics were big business in the 4th century and really boomed in the notoriously superstitious Middle Ages.

Almost simultaneously, a blog on the *Christianity Today* website pointed out that the Knights Templar are still looking for the Holy Grail, only today they are using ultrasound and thermal imaging to search beneath the 15th century Rosslyn Chapel near Edinburgh, Scotland. The Knights Templar date back to the Crusades. The Holy Grail is thought to be the cup from which Jesus served the first communion, and in which Joseph of Arimathea caught the blood of Jesus dripping from the cross. The quest for the Holy Grail was the highest spiritual pursuit in the King Arthur legends. Finding it depended not only on locating it, but of being of pure heart.

These reports not only reflect an inability to separate fact from fiction, but also illustrate our human nature and our desire to define spirituality on our own terms. Both stories fit the spirit of the *Da Vinci Code*.[1] The people at that Toronto Church thought that the splinter of what they thought was the cross of Christ somehow had power to bring them closer to Christ. The person who stole it thought it had resale value to someone else. Those Knights Templar searching for the Holy Grail see in it spiritual power.

But there is a better way to draw close to Jesus. It is not found in the exotic but in the common. If all the pieces of the cross that were sold in the Middle Ages could be collected together, you could probably build a thousand crosses from them. And if the Holy Grail were found and filled, not everyone could taste of it before the end of the age. But Jesus made a better way. He instituted the Lord's Supper so that everyone everywhere every time they wanted could eat and drink and find strength and closeness to Jesus, not from the vessel from which they drink or the cross that bore His body, but from the living presence of Jesus who is with us as we eat and drink.

> The Lord Jesus, on the night he was betrayed, took bread, and when he had given thanks, he broke it and said, "This is my body, which is for you; do this is remembrance of me." In the same way, after supper he took the cup saying, "This cup is the new covenant in my blood; do this whenever you drink it, in remembrance of me." (1 Cor 11:23-25)

Prayer

Lord, in our eating and drinking, our desire is not for a splinter of the cross or a view of the chalice but in the bread and in the cup, we seek only you—to remember you and to know you—next to which everything else is foolishness. Amen.

More to Consider

How does the Lord's Supper bring you closer to Jesus? Can you imagine a better way to accomplish this?

---

[1]Dan Brown, *The Da Vinci Code* (New York: Doubleday, 2003).

37

REMEMBERING ESSENTIAL TRUTHS

ORLD YOUTH DAY attracts hundreds of thousands of Catholic young people from all over the world. When held in Cologne, Germany, the Germans had to process somewhere near a million visas. They were worried about dealing with these large numbers and they were worried about illegal aliens, especially Muslims, slipping into the country, so they developed a test to fast track these young people seeking a visa. They asked them, among other things, to name the seven sacraments and the seven deadly sins—these are, no doubt, part of Catholic catechism and any Catholic young person should know the answers to them. Then they asked them how and when Jesus died. They might have added another element to 'how and when." They might have added "why." At any rate, I think the reason for the question is that Muslims do not believe Jesus was crucified and believe that He died at age 120.

Even if it was only meant to trip up Muslims, the question is intriguing. What is the single most important doctrinal question for Christians? We are not saved by knowledge. We are saved by grace, but surely our knowledge about the death of Jesus is essential to our being Christians. In fact, the one lesson that Jesus left His church to be taught over and over was the lesson about His death, which is reenacted in the two ordinances

He left His church—baptism and the Lord's Supper. Every Sunday, we are to remember, at the Lord's Table, His death by crucifixion, about 30 AD, outside the city of Jerusalem, as a sacrifice for our sins. And we learn what it says about who He is, why He came to this world, what our relationship to Him is, why He was raised from the dead, and perhaps all the essential truths of the faith.

> While they were eating, Jesus took bread, and when he had given thanks, he broke it and gave it to his disciples, saying, "Take and eat; this is my body." Then he took a cup, and when he had given thanks, he gave it to them, saying, "Drink from it, all of you. This is my blood of the covenant, which is poured out for many for the forgiveness of sins."　　　　　　　　　　　　　　　　(Matt 26:26-28)

PRAYER

Lord, we do not understand all we know about your death on the cross, but we remember your death on the cross as the greatest event in human history and the greatest event in our own experience and we thank you. Amen.

MORE TO CONSIDER

Think about what you know about the death of Jesus. How would you articulate your understanding to others?

38

A Room
Called Remember Him

I N ONE OF his books, preacher and author Frederick Buechner tells of a dream he once had. He dreamed he was staying in a hotel somewhere and he stayed in a room he loved. He does not remember what it looked like, but he remembers the way it made him feel—happy and at peace. He left there, went places and did things, then he came back to the hotel. He was given a different room in which he felt dark and cramped. He finally went to the man at the desk and told him that he did not like his room, but he had had a room on an earlier visit that he loved, and he would like to have that room. The problem was that he did not know where the room was. He did not know how to find it or ask for it. The clerk was very understanding and told him he knew exactly which room it was, and it was available. He told him that the next time he visited, he should ask for it by name. Buechner asked him the name and he answered that it was a room called remember.

Buechner says that shocked him awake. He pondered on the meaning of the dream and concluded that there could be healing and blessing in remembering. He concluded that the important memories were not those nostalgic, poignant, or even terrible memories brought on by an old photograph or a song or a place or sound or smell. It was intentional memories about the important events of our lives that have made us what we are and brought us to where we are. Despite all the memories, both very good and very bad, we have survived, and this truth gives us peace and to quote Buechner, "a sense that in some unfathomable way all is well."

With this in mind, leave the place where you are at this particular moment and enter into a *Room Called Remember Him.* You can enter it anytime at will. Come in and remember the events of your life that made you what you are and brought you to where you are. Especially take time to remember Jesus and His involvement. In doing so, you will come to the place where your path crosses His, the place of the cross. Remember that it is because of Jesus that you can have peace and "a sense that in some unfathomable way all is well." "Everyone ought to examine themselves before they eat of the bread and drink from the cup" (1 Cor 11:28), writes Paul. Jesus says, "do this in remembrance of me" (1 Cor 11:24).

PRAYER

Our Father, the memories of our lives are both good and bad, but the memory of what Jesus did for us is immeasurably good. This morning as we eat and drink, we remember. Amen.

MORE TO CONSIDER

What events in your life have made you who you are? Do you feel that God was at work in them? And if so, in what way?

39

THE GREATNESS OF JESUS

THE LORD'S SUPPER provides a recurring opportunity to remember the greatest life that was ever lived and the greatest thing that was ever done. Consider this:

- About 100 million Bibles—books about Jesus—were distributed in 2022.[1] His life is the subject and purpose of the Bible—both the Old Testament, of which He said, "These are the very Scriptures that testify about me" (John 5:39), and the New Testament, which tells us all we know about Him.

- Jesus claimed to be God in the flesh, and the people who knew Him believed Him.

- With 2.38 billion followers, He is the founder of the world's largest religion.[2]

- According to an internet search program that scours the web for opinions about famous people, He is the most important person in history.[3]

- He is the inspiration for the finest music, art, and literature in human history.

- As of 2020, 109 million books have been written about Him.[4] It is unlikely that that many books are in print on any other subject.

- His coming into the world has long been the dividing point of our calendar. Before He came it was B.C. (Before Christ) after He came it is A.D. (anno domini—the year of our Lord).

Jesus is no doubt the greatest man that ever lived. But more importantly, He did the greatest thing that was ever done:

- Though present at the foundation of the world and involved in the creation of all things, He left the glory of heaven to come to earth and be God with us.

- While here, He healed the sick, fed the hungry, raised the dead, calmed the storm, and walked on water.

- He taught with the authority of God, showed the love of God, and represented the grace of God.

- But the greatest thing He ever did was to die on the cross for the forgiveness of the sin of the world.

So, take a moment to remember the greatest man who ever lived doing the greatest thing that was ever done.

PRAYER

Lord, may we never participate in the Lord's Supper or come before you in prayer without sincere gratitude and proper respect for who Jesus is and what He has done, for as Paul wrote to the Colossians, He is "the image of the invisible God, the firstborn over all creation" (Col 1:15). Amen.

MORE TO CONSIDER

For more on the supremacy of Christ, read Colossians 1:15-23. What is your favorite thing to remember about the life of Jesus?

---

[1]Adam Phillips, "How Many Bibles are Sold Each Year? Unveiling Annual Sales Data," The Witness, September 1, 2023. https://thewitness.org/how-many-bibles-are-sold-each-year/

[2]World Population Review, accessed January 15, 2024. https://worldpopulationreview.com/country-rankings/religion-by-country.

[3]"How Jesus is most famous person in history...and Cameron is only 1,483rd according to internet searches," Daily Mail, December 14, 2013. https://www.dailymail.co.uk/news/article-2523930/Jesus-famous-person-history-according-software-algorithm.html

[4]"Guess Who Leads The Top 10 People Books Have Been Written About," HillFaith, 2021. https://www.hillfaith.org/bible/guess-who-heads-the-list-of-the-top-10-people-authors-have-written-books-about/.

THE BREAD AND CUP
AS SYMBOLS

40   Ordinary Symbols of Extraordinary Meaning. 101

41   The Bread of Affliction and Cup of Redemption 103

42   The Best of Many 105

43   From the Inside Out 107

44   Beyond Description. 109

45   Foreshadowing a Future Banquet 113

46   An Unexpected Pardon 115

THE BREAD AND CUP OF COMMUNION are the symbols that Jesus chose to represent His body and blood and to remind His followers of His sacrifice for them. These symbols, as part of the traditional Passover feast, were already meaningful to the Jews of Jesus' day. The meditations of this section explore both the reason for and meaning of the chosen symbols, and mention a number of other symbols that could have been selected.

40

ORDINARY SYMBOLS OF EXTRAORDINARY MEANING

W HEN JESUS wanted to get an important message across to the people around Him, He did not give them a complicated explanation. He told them a story, a story about a father who had two sons, or about a Samaritan who helped a Jew.[1] And when He wanted His followers to remember the most important event of His life on earth, He chose two ordinary items, bread and wine, and used them as symbols for His body and blood.

Addressing the apostles in the upper room,

> ...he took bread, gave thanks and broke it, and gave it to them saying, "This is my body given for you; do this in remembrance of me." In the same way, after the supper he took the cup, saying, "This cup is the new covenant in my blood, which is poured out for you."
>
> (Luke 22:19-20)

Jesus chose symbols and words that focus our attention on His humanity—His body. And on this simple belief—that His death somehow set things right between God and us, giving us a fresh start.[2] That is why He had a body. That is what He came to earth to do. If His incarnation was a miracle, if the virgin birth was a miracle, if His resurrection and ascension were miracles, then surely the greatest miracle is all those miracles working together to somehow make things right between God and us. If we had a perfect understanding of how that was done, it would not be miraculous. So, on the eve of His crucifixion, Jesus did not give us a complicated explanation of precisely how His death could wash away our sins. He gave us two ordinary items, bread and wine, to remind us that it did.

PRAYER

We thank you for Jesus' ability to make the complex and mysterious seem simple and within reach. We thank you for His willingness to take human form and sacrifice His body and blood so that we could be made right with you. Whenever we share the bread and cup, accept our humble efforts to remember and honor your Son, in whose name we pray. Amen.

MORE TO CONSIDER

Consider the Parable of the Good Samaritan (Luke 10:25-37) and the Parable of the Prodigal Son (Luke 15:11-32). Do they help you understand the ideas that Jesus is trying to convey? How do the bread and cup do that with respect to communion?

---

[1]This observation was made in the notes of Rowland Croucher (http://jmm.aaa.au/articles/2295.htm) on a sermon preached at *Syndal Baptist Church*, June 7, 1997. Rowland Croucher, "A Communion Meditation," John Mark Ministries, January 4, 2003, https://www.jmm.org.au/articles/2295.htm.

[2]C. S. Lewis, *Mere Christianity* (New York: Simon & Schuster, 1996), 58.

41

THE BREAD OF AFFLICTION
AND CUP OF REDEMPTION

W HAT JESUS DID on the occasion of the institution of the Lord's Supper was not the most important thing that happened in that upper room. He had gathered there with the twelve apostles for a memorial. He ate the ceremonial bread. He drank the ceremonial cups. He did what Jews had been doing for centuries. The memorial was to the departure of the Jews from Israel under the leadership of Moses. The bread was, as the head of the household would quote, "The *bread of affliction* that our fathers ate in the land of Egypt."[1] The participants in the Passover drank four cups, each of which had a symbolic meaning to the Jews. The third one was the *Cup of Redemption*. It symbolized the blood of the Passover lamb.

What Jesus did in the upper room was what Jews had been doing for centuries. It was what He said that made all the difference. He took the bread "and when he had given thanks, he broke it and gave it to his disciples," and instead of saying, "This is the bread of affliction,"[1] He said, "Take and eat, this is my body" (Matt 26:26). He took the third cup, the one symbolizing the blood of the lamb, but He did not quote from Exodus, "I will redeem you with an outstretched arm and with mighty acts of judgment" (Exod 6:6). Instead, He said "Drink from it all of you. This is my blood of the New Covenant, which is poured out for many for the

103

forgiveness of sins" (Matt 26:27-28). And when redefining the cherished memorial to the Exodus, He said "Do this in remembrance of me" (1 Cor 11:24).

So, it was not so much what Jesus did in the upper room that matters. It was all about what He said. The memorial was no longer to be about the bread of affliction. It was no longer to be about the blood of the lamb. It was no longer about remembering the Exodus. From that moment on, it was all about Jesus. So, we now remember Him.

PRAYER

Our Father, we understand that the whole of the Old Testament, every symbol, every shadow, every type is about Jesus. With the bread and the cup, we celebrate the new meaning that He gave to everything when He died and rose again and promised the same for us. We remember and we thank you in Jesus' name. Amen.

MORE TO CONSIDER

Do the bread and the cup give meaning to your life?

---

[1]Rabbi Danielle Upbin, "Ha Lachma Anya: The Bread of Slavery and Affliction," My Jewish Learning, April 4, 2019, https://www.myjewishlearning.com/article/ha-lachma-anya-the-bread-of-slavery-and-affliction/#:~:text=This%20is%20the%20bread%20of%20affliction%20that%20our%20ancestors%20ate,we%20will%20be%20free%20people.

42

THE BEST OF MANY

D O THIS in remembrance of me.[1] Though a simple request, the circumstances under which it was made were not so simple. Jesus, who is, and was, and always will be,[2] was preparing Himself and His disciples for something He had never experienced before; something He would never experience again. A once-and-for-all kind of death that would wash away our sin and, in the process, separate Him from God, His Father, for the first and only time in all of eternity. And though He surely knew that there would be a resurrection, that He would be reunited with His Father, and that He would be forever present with His earthly followers through the Holy Spirit, He still wanted us to remember the final moments of His life as a man. There are other things that Jesus could have asked us to remember:

- He could have asked us to remember His teachings. We all love knowledge. In fact, we equate knowledge with power, and we want our children to gain as much knowledge as possible.

- He could have asked us to remember His miracles. Everyone loves miracles. As the success of movies based on books like *Harry Potter*[3] and *The Lord of the Rings*[4] demonstrate, people are fascinated by the supernatural.

- He could have asked us to remember His Father. He was always deflecting attention from Himself to the Father. There is a certain mystery there, for "no one has ever seen God" (John 1:18), and we love a good mystery.

But He asked us to remember His body and blood—His death. They teach us something that doctrines and miracles and our natural wonder of God cannot. Like clothes that you are unwilling to purchase until you have tried them on, Jesus put His teachings, miracles, and relationship with God on, and in His death, showed us how we are to live.

PRAYER

Father, Jesus gave us the bread and cup of communion to remind us of His physical body, which was sacrificed for us on the cross, and His blood, which was poured out for the forgiveness of our sin. His life and death define obedience, submission, love, and service. Help us to follow His example in our relationships with both you and one another. Amen.

MORE TO CONSIDER

Do the bread and cup remind you of the humanity of Jesus and the perfect faith and behavior that He modeled? Does his example of faith make you want to emulate Him?

---

[1]See Luke 22:19.

[2]See Rev 1:4.

[3]J.K. Rowling, *Harry Potter* (UK: Bloomsbury Publishing, 1997-2007).

[4]J.R.R. Tolkien, *Lord of the Rings* (UK: Allen and Urwin, 1954-1955).

43

FROM THE INSIDE OUT

I N 1775, the year before our Declaration of Independence, General Benedict Arnold was preparing to lead colonial troops to Quebec to enlist Canadians in the American cause—or if necessary, to defeat them. Before leaving, Arnold's chaplain, Samuel Spring, had an idea for motivating the troops. He marched them to Newburyport, Massachusetts, to the grave of a famous preacher named George Whitfield. They dug up the casket, broke it open, and removed from the skeleton Whitfield's clerical collar and wristbands. Spring cut them up and distributed them among the troops for inspiration. People need something to remind them of what is important, something to stir their memories.[1]

On the night when He was betrayed, Jesus gave the apostles something by which to remember Him. He could have given them a cross carved from a dogwood tree to wear around their necks, or a pin to wear on their garments like a Jewish phylactery. A more permanent reminder would have been a tattoo—perhaps the word Jesus or Lord on the back of their right hands. The early Christians used the symbol of a fish to identify one another. The Greek word for fish is "ichthys" and those letters stand for "Jesus Christ, Son of God, Savior." One could find Biblical support for any of these symbols. All could have been have used as reminders of Jesus' death, but He chose something different because remembrances like these are external in nature and He wanted something internal. In other words:

- The Christian faith is not something to be put *on* you but something to be put *in* you.

- It is not a symbol to be seen by others, but a life to be lived before the world.

- It is not a one-time event, but a regular renewal.

- It is not an individual act, but a community celebration.

So, when Jesus gave His apostles the cup and the loaf, it was as if to say, Christianity is something to be taken internally:

- The bread is to feed your soul.

- The fruit of the vine is to flow through your veins.

- In other words, "unless you eat the flesh of the Son of Man and drink his blood, you have no life in you" (John 6:53).

Rather than thinking of communion as looking back to the Passover, we should think of the Passover as preparing for the day when Jesus would eat communion with His disciples in the upper room. And the day when we would take the Lord's Supper in remembrance of Him and become more like Him from the inside out.

PRAYER

Our Father, we know that life in the fullness of Christ begins with a change of heart and attitude—it begins on the inside. May the bread and cup remind us of Christ's physical sacrifice for us and that it was meant to change us from the inside out. Amen.

MORE TO CONSIDER

Have you ever considered the communion emblems as bread to feed your soul and blood to flow through your veins? What does that mean to you?

---

[1]Kenneth E. Lawson, "Rev. George Whitefield's Influence on Colonial Chaplains in the American Revolution," Journal of the American Revolution, Feburary 16, 2022, https://allthingsliberty.com/2022/02/rev-george-whitefields-influence-on-colonial-chaplains-in-the-american-revolution/.

44

BEYOND DESCRIPTION

I N ISAIAH 55:9, God said, "As the heavens are higher than the Earth, so are my ways higher than your ways and my thoughts [*higher*] than your thoughts" (Isa 55:9). No wonder the Bible is filled with figurative language:

- God is a fortress that protects, a potter that molds, the Alpha and the Omega.[1]

- God's word is a lamp that shines, a mirror that reveals, a sword that pierces, a fire that consumes.[2]

- The Holy Spirit is a wind that blows, a breath that infuses.[3]

- Satan is a roaring lion that devours.[4]

- The church is a bride, the kingdom of God is a treasure hidden in a field, hell is a lake of fire.[5]

Virtually every reference to God and His kingdom in the Bible is metaphorical. And in some cases—like in Ezekiel, Zechariah, and Revelation—the imagery is beyond comprehension.

Jesus stands out as the one tangible manifestation of the divine that could be seen and touched and questioned and learned from. And even He described Himself metaphorically:

- 'I am the light of the world" (John 9:5).

- 'I am the vine" (John 15:5).

- 'I am the good shepherd" (John 10:11).

- 'I am the bread of life" (John 6:35).

- 'I am the way and the truth and the life" (John 14:6).

He left our world as the good shepherd who had laid down His life for His sheep. But not before giving us one last metaphor to contemplate—the bread and cup of communion.

The bread, of course, is His body, the bread of life. He once said, 'my flesh is real food" (John 6:55). It nourishes us. And like the Passover bread that was used to commemorate the Exodus, the bread of communion reminds us that His body purchased our freedom from sin.

The wine is his blood.[6] And wine is the fruit of the vine that He pictured himself to be. We are the branches of that vine and the recipients of its life-giving blood—a blood that sealed the covenant of grace that He secured on the cross. So, as you eat the bread, drink from the cup, and construct your own mental picture of what they mean, consider the metaphors of Jesus and recall that He also said,

> **Whoever eats my flesh and drinks my blood has eternal life, and I will raise him up at the last day.** (John 6:54)

PRAYER

Father, you are beyond our description. John aptly called your Son the 'Lamb of God" (John 1:36), a metaphor that emphasizes his role as the sacrifice for our sin. We remember that sacrifice now and thank you for it in Jesus' name. Amen.

MORE TO CONSIDER

How would you describe Jesus? Is there a metaphor that makes the most sense to you?

---

[1]See Psalm 18:2, 84:11; Isaiah 64:8; Revelation 21:6.

[2]See 1 John 3:16; James 1:23; Hebrews 4:12-13; James 1:23.

[3]See John 3:7-8, Acts 2:2-4; John 20:19-20, 22, Job 3:4.

[4]See 1 Peter 5:8.

[5]See Revelation 19:7, Matthew 13:44, Revelation 20:14.

[6]It is commonly assumed that wine was used at the Lord's Supper. However, many churches use grape juice instead and it is also a fruit of the vine.

45

FORESHADOWING
A FUTURE BANQUET

AT THE CONCLUSION of Matthew's account of the Passover Feast culminating in the Lord's Supper, Jesus makes a promise to His disciples that He will drink of the fruit of the vine again with them in His Father's kingdom. Consider Matthew's account:

> While they were eating, Jesus took bread, and when he had given thanks, he broke it and gave it to his disciples, saying, "Take and eat; this is my body." Then he took a cup, and when he had given thanks, he gave it to them, saying, "Drink from it, all of you. This is my blood of the covenant, which is poured out for many for the forgiveness of sins. I tell you, I will not drink from this fruit of the vine from now on until that day when I drink it new with you in my Father's kingdom."
> (Matt 26:26-29)

Many believe that the event Jesus describes as drinking it with you in His Father's kingdom refers to the wedding supper of the Lamb as described in Revelation 19:9. The feast is often mentioned in the Gospels as the great event at the consummation or completion of the Kingdom. Reflect on what Jesus says about that *Great Banquet* in the following parable:

> When one of those at the table with him heard this, he said to Jesus, "Blessed is the one who will eat at the feast in the kingdom of God."

113

Jesus replied: "A certain man was preparing a great banquet and invited many guests. At the time of the banquet, he sent his servant to tell those who had been invited, 'Come, for everything is now ready.' But they all alike began to make excuses.... The servant came back and reported this to his master. Then the owner of the house became angry and ordered his servant, 'Go out quickly into the streets and alleys of the town and bring in the poor, the crippled, the blind and the lame.' 'Sir,' the servant said, 'what you ordered has been done, but there is still room.' Then the master told his servant, 'Go out to the roads and country lanes and compel them [by persuasion] to come in, so that my house will be full. I tell you, not one of those who were invited will get a taste of my banquet.'"

(Luke 14:15-24)

This may be read as Jesus' rejection of the Jews and his invitation to the Gentiles, who were considered helpless and hopeless, to the Kingdom, but it *also* certainly is a parable about persuading those who need the Gospel to respond to the invitation. The invitation is to come to the banquet. You come to the banquet by coming to Christ. With this in mind, any invitation to the Lord's Supper might include the words *banquet to follow.*

PRAYER

Our Father, as we eat the bread and drink the cup, we remember the Lord's death and we remember the reason for it. We pray for millions around the world to join us at this table with the promise that we will join Him at that table when the great banquet is spread. Let it be so in Jesus' name. Amen.

MORE TO CONSIDER

Do your think that the Lord's Supper foreshadows the great banquet that is mentioned in Revelation? If so, not only are the bread and cup symbols of Jesus' body and blood, but communion itself is a symbol of a banquet to come. Does that reality add new meaning to the Lord's Supper for you?

46

AN UNEXPECTED PARDON

FYODOR DOSTOEVSKY, a 19th Century Russian writer who is best known for his books *Crime and Punishment* and *The Brothers Karamazov*, lived an interesting life.[1]

As a young man, Dostoevsky was arrested for belonging to a group considered treasonous by the Czar. While awaiting sentencing in prison, he was removed from his cell and carted to the town square, where he received the unreasonable and completely unexpected sentence of death. He had no time to think and no way to appeal. The firing squad was ready. Robed in a white burial shroud, hands tied behind his back, he was paraded to the place of execution.

"The wages of sin is death" (Rom 6:23), the clerk said, and then offered him a cross to kiss. He was tied to a post. Rifles were cocked and shouldered. Drums rumbled. The words that we sometimes associate with communion, "a man ought to examine himself" (1 Cor 11:28), may have gone through his mind. As a young man, Dostoevsky's whole life was before him; he had plans, dreams, a purpose. All would be lost. He may have kissed the cross, but he had no real faith.

Just as the sound of the guns being cocked reached his ears, a horseman came galloping up, and according to a prearranged plan of the Czar, commuted his sentence to hard labor. A sentence of hard labor was never so well received. He later wrote to his brother, "I shall be born again in a new form." From that day forward, his life had new meaning.

Three days later, on a Christmas Day, Dostoevsky was transported on an 18-day trip in an open horse drawn sledge to a Siberian prison. Upon arrival, he met a woman whose husband was a political prisoner, but who had permission to comfort arriving prisoners. She gave him a New Testament, the only book that was allowed in the prison. Search it carefully, she told him, and he later found ten rubles hidden in it. After ten years in prison with that New Testament, he emerged with an unshakable faith in Christ.

On another occasion, as he was walking along a street with a guard, a little girl came running up to him crying, "There, poor unfortunate, take a kopek in the name of Christ."

All three events impacted Dostoevsky's life. He kept the white burial shroud to remind him of the day he virtually came back from the dead, the Bible wherein he found the meaning of life, and the coin that reminded him of the grace of God. The bread and cup of the Lord's Supper are more ordinary than the things that Dostoevsky kept, but the things we remember are equally profound. The bread and the juice remind us, among other things, of Jesus' life, His love, His grace, His sacrifice, His promises, and of our new life.

PRAYER

Father, though we may not muster the same intensity of feeling that Dostoevsky felt when his sentence was commuted, we have received an even greater pardon—an amazing grace that was made possible by the sacrifice of Jesus. We thank you for that in His name. Amen.

MORE TO CONSIDER

Have you ever felt the kind of relief that Dostoevsky experienced? Was it when you found out that Jesus took your place on the cross? Do the bread and cup remind you of that?

---

[1]Philip Yancey, *Soul Survivor* (Colorado Springs: Waterbrook Press, 2001), 134-138.

THE ART OR PRACTICE OF REMEMBERING

47   Communing in Prayer 119
48   On Being Worthy. 123
49   Worship Lessons 125
50   Communion as Worship. 127
51   The Shadow of the Cup. 129
52   Remembered by Jesus 131
53   Our First Response. 133
54   Putting Yourself Ahead of God 135
55   Examining Yourself. 137
56   The Hands of Betrayers. 139
57   A Comforting Memorial. 141
58   Father, Son, Holy Spirit, and You 143
59   Assessing Your Love of God. 145
60   A Fresh Start. 147
61   Unity in Christ 149
62   Rededication 151

COMMUNION MEDITATIONS are designed to direct the thoughts of those participating in a communion service to a particular aspect of Jesus' life and death on the cross. But *communing* is more than just thinking about the content of a prepared meditation. It normally involves prayer, worship, and self-examination, at the very least.

The meditations in this section present a variety of ways to approach the communion experience. The first mediation, *Communing in Prayer*, illustrates communing through prayer and is based on Jesus' words of institution from Luke 22. *The Shadow of the Cup*, on the other hand, addresses the mindset of communion participants. Other meditations focus on methods of self-examination, something that Paul asked the Corinthians to do in 1 Corinthians 11. Together, these meditations explore a range of topics related to the art or practice of remembering—the experience of communion itself. See also *How to Remember*[1] in the section entitled *The Purpose of the Lord's Supper*.

[1]Meditation 32.

47

COMMUNING IN PRAYER

OUR FATHER IN HEAVEN,

We come to you as one in heart and mind,
  created in your image,
  deformed by our sin,
  restored by your Son,
  and knowing that through it all, you have desired to
      commune with us.
  We offer ourselves as eager communicants,
  remembering that Jesus, who died to mend our
      relationship with you,
  said to His disciples and to us through them:

"I have eagerly desired to eat this Passover with you."
(Luke 22:14)

We come to you, Father, as a people who want to serve you,
  knowing that you hold the whole world in your hands,
  and that there is no safer place than under your will.
  With the help of your Spirit,
  we offer you our bodies, as living sacrifices,

119

remembering that Jesus, who set aside the privileges of
deity to become a man,
said to His disciples and to us through them:

"This is my body given for you." (Luke 22:19)

We come to you, Father, as undeserving sinners,
knowing that we have all made our own mistakes in our
own ways,
but that the solution is always the same, your forgiveness.
We offer you our repentance, and our gratitude that we
are no longer under the law, but under your grace.
We remember that Jesus is our mediator in the covenant
of grace,
and that He said to His disciples and to us through them:

*"This cup is the new covenant in my blood, which is poured
out for you."* (Luke 22:20)

And we come to you, Father, knowing that we have a tendency
to forget,
to be caught up in the world itself, and to take you, the
creator and sustainer of the world, for granted.
We offer you this moment,
as we reflect upon your goodness and power and mercy
and grace,
and on the suffering and crucifixion and resurrection of
your Son,
remembering that He Himself, on the night that He was
betrayed,
took bread and wine and said to His disciples and to us
through them:

"Do this in remembrance of me." (Luke 22:19)

As we share these symbols of the bread and wine that
Jesus shared with His disciples, we offer you our
prayers in the name of our Lord Jesus Christ. Amen.

MORE TO CONSIDER

What do you pray about when participating in the Lord's Supper? Is it about the sacrifice of Jesus and your response to it?

48

ON BEING WORTHY

I N 2ND THESSALONIANS, the apostle Paul prayed that the Thessalonians would "be counted worthy of the kingdom of God" and of God's "calling" (2 Thess 1:5,11). To be counted worthy is the desire of every Christian. But if you have ever asked yourself, "Am I worthy of God's favor?" you may have concluded that you are not. In fact, you probably concluded that you are not. We are all a lot like the prodigal son, who after disappointing his father, said, "I am no longer worthy to be called your son" (Luke 15:19).

On more than one occasion, Jesus spoke about being worthy. He once told a parable, for example, about a Pharisee and the tax collector. The Pharisee prayed about himself, thanking God that he was not like other men. The tax collector "would not even look up to heaven, but beat his breast and said, 'God, have mercy on me, a sinner'" (Luke 18:9-14). According to Jesus, the tax collector—the one who clearly felt unworthy—went home justified before God.

And in the Sermon on the Mount, Jesus said, "Blessed are the poor in spirit, for theirs is the kingdom of heaven" (Matt 5:3). Who are the poor in spirit? They are those who know that they have nothing within themselves to commend them to God.[1] Yet paradoxically, recognizing their own poverty—or spiritual unworthiness—somehow makes them worthy of the kingdom of heaven.

So, when you take the bread and cup of communion, if you feel unworthy of the sacrifice that they represent, thank God that you are not putting your faith in yourself, but in the one of whom scripture says, "Worthy is the Lamb, who was slain" (Rev 5:12). Just like the prodigal son, who felt unworthy but was nevertheless welcomed by his father, so too God welcomes us when we put our trust in the broken body and shed blood of Jesus, who is the worthy lamb that was slain.

PRAYER

Father, our feelings of unworthiness always seem to increase when we take the bread and cup and think about the sacrifice that Jesus made on our behalf. We are unworthy of your favor; we know that we cannot earn our salvation. We can only praise you and thank you again for your Son and for His worthiness and for the grace that He made possible through His death on a cross. Amen.

MORE TO CONSIDER

Does feeling worthy indicate that you will be found worthy? Or conversely, is the only way to disqualify yourself from the fellowship of Jesus to think that you do not need Him?

---

[1]R. Kent Hughes, *The Sermon on the Mount: The Message of the Kingdom* (Wheaton: Crossway Books, 2001), 13-24.

49

WORSHIP LESSONS

A THOUSAND YEARS BEFORE Jesus was born, God's chosen people practiced a sacrificial form of worship in a temple that was designed and commissioned by God. And over time, because of the emptiness of their rituals, God inspired the prophet Amos to write:

> I despise your religious festivals... Away with the noise of your songs!
> (Amos 5:21-23)

They had somehow missed the point of worship.

After the temple was destroyed and the Jews were scattered across the Middle East, they began to worship in local, man-made synagogues. And rather than sacrificing animals, they emphasized an inward sacrifice of the heart, primarily through prayer and a study of the Law. But just like in the temple, their worship eventually began to displease God. And when Jesus arrived on the scene and saw them in their synagogues, He called them hypocrites, and questioned their motives for everything from fasting to giving to prayer.

> "Be careful", he said, "not to do your acts of righteousness in front of others, to be seen by them. If you do, you will have no reward from your Father in heaven." (Matt 6:1)

God was still not satisfied with their worship.

After Jesus was crucified and resurrected and had ascended to Heaven, Christ-followers began to worship in houses. According to Acts, "They devoted themselves to the apostles' teaching and to the fellowship, to the breaking of bread and to prayer" (Acts 2:42). Their focus was now the sacrifice of Jesus, but even they found ways to pervert their worship. Some took the Lord's Supper in an unworthy manner and that caused the apostle Paul to write: "your meetings do more harm than good" (1 Cor 11:17).

> **Everyone ought to examine themselves before they eat of the bread and drink from the cup. For those who eat and drink without discerning the body of Christ eat and drink judgment on themselves.**
>
> **(1 Cor 11:28-29)**

It seems that the more things changed, the more they stayed the same.

We, of course, are not in a temple or a synagogue or a home, but it has never been enough to just *be present* at any place or time of worship, or to just go through the motions, or to take part with the wrong motives, or in a careless, self-centered way. So, avoid those mistakes whenever and wherever you worship.

PRAYER

Father, we, like our predecessors, are prone to sin, even in our worship. So, as we take the bread and cup in recognition of the body and blood that was sacrificed for us, help us to worship in a manner that is worthy of the sacrifice we are remembering. Amen.

MORE TO CONSIDER

Have you fallen into any of the traps that the early Jews and Christians did? Can you think of ways to reduce the temptation to do so?

50

COMMUNION AS WORSHIP

IN 2008, a program called *Faith in Action* was sponsored by several leading evangelical organizations. The program proposed that churches cancel their Sunday worship on what it called "Outreach Sunday" so their members could engage in some sort of community service. "A church that puts its faith into action focuses not on themselves, but on Christ's teaching and His divine example of compassion," said the promoters. "Our hope is that churches across the country will unite to show their community a true servant's heart."

It was probably inevitable that some would so trivialize worship that they would want to do something on Sunday morning that *mattered*. Not much became of Outreach Sunday, and it is just as well. It was a bad idea from the start:

- It was bad because Sunday morning is not a very good time to do community service— whatever that is.

- It was bad because it implied that church members only give one or two hours a week to serve Christ, and that on Sunday morning. How about a Saturday community service day?

- And it was bad, above all, because it denied the importance of what goes on at church on Sunday morning.

When the church comes together to study, worship, hear the Word of God, and meet at the Lord's table, *it is putting faith into action.* Communal worship does not keep us from Christian service; it prepares us for it. Spending time at the Lord's table reminds us of what our faith is all about:

> For I received from the Lord what I also passed on to you: the Lord Jesus, on the night he was betrayed, took bread, and when he had given thanks, he broke it and said, "This is my body, which is for you; do this in remembrance of me." In the same way, after supper he took the cup, saying, "This cup is the new covenant in my blood; do this, whenever you drink it, in remembrance of me." For whenever you eat this bread and drink this cup, you proclaim the Lord's death until he comes. (1 Cor 11:23-26)

Prayer

Our Father, we come before you in worship as an expression of our faith. While our worship is simple, we do not consider it trivial. While the loaf and cup are plain, we do not consider them common. In our community worship, we consider ourselves uniquely in your presence. In partaking of the loaf and cup, we consider ourselves singularly blessed by communion with you. Help us never doubt the importance of what we do here, as we remember the death of Jesus and His life in us. Give your blessing to the loaf and the cup and those who participate. Amen.

More to Consider

Are worship services important to you? Do you make it a point to be a part of them? Do you view the Lord's Supper as an act of worship?

51

THE SHADOW OF THE CUP

Drink from it, all of you. This is my blood of the covenant, which is poured out for many for the forgiveness of sins.   (Matt 26:27-28)

S OME PEOPLE look at a half a cup and say it is half full, and others say it is half empty. Whether you consider the cup half full or half empty is supposed to say something about you, but sometimes it says something about the circumstances. In the same way:

- Some come to the communion table reflecting on the sadness of the death of Jesus, and others come rejoicing at the benefits of the death of Jesus.

- Some take the loaf broken hearted by His broken body, and others take the loaf uplifted by His resurrected body.

- Some drink the cup rejoicing that His blood cleanses us from all sin. Others drink grief-stricken that their sins caused the shedding of His sacrificial blood.

The truth is that the blood and body of Jesus are occasions for both sorrow and for rejoicing.

Imagine a man needing a heart transplant to live. His son is killed in a tragic accident and the father receives the son's heart. His joy is immeasurable because he will live, but his misery is unfathomable because his son died. So, we come to the Lord's table and our cup is at the same time half full and half empty.

- We know *we live* because He died.

- We know we live because *He died.*

We live under the shadow of the cup. We recognize it when we participate in the Lord's Supper.

PRAYER

There is no way to express, our Father, our sadness because of the death of Jesus or our joy because of the death of Jesus. Our meditation is bittersweet. Overflowing with gratitude, we remember. Overcome with sorrow, we remember. In Jesus name. Amen.

MORE TO CONSIDER

How do you feel when participating in communion? Do you see the cup as half full or half empty?

52

REMEMBERED BY JESUS

OD WANTS us to remember. So, we find the word "remember" throughout our Bibles. We find it in passages that tell us how to live, like "remember to help the poor" (Gal 2:10 NLT) and "remember to live peaceably with each other" (1 Thess 5:13 NLT). We find it in admonitions and warnings, like "Remember what happened to Lot's wife" (Luke 17:32 NLT) and "Remember, it is sin to know what you ought to do and then not do it" (Jas 4:17 NLT). And we find it in scripture whose purpose is to commemorate, like "Remember to observe the Sabbath day by keeping it holy" (Exod 20:8 NLT) and "do this in remembrance of me" (Luke 22:19).

Time after time, God instructs us to remember. But in the 23rd chapter of Luke, we find a man who desperately wants *God to remember.* While witnessing firsthand the breaking of Jesus' body and the shedding of His blood, one of the criminals being crucified at His side turns to Jesus and pleads, "remember me when you come into your kingdom" (Luke 23:42).

Imagine that man's desperation. He was a sinner on the verge of death and eternal punishment coming to the realization that Jesus is the key to life. And imagine his relief when Jesus replies, "Truly I tell you, today you will be with me in paradise" (Luke 23:43). It is not hard to imagine:

- We have all, if taking communion today, come to the same realization.

- We have all felt the same relief.

- And we all want to be remembered by Jesus.

So, this morning, as the bread and the cup make their way to you, remember God's Son, remember His broken body, His shed blood, His promise of paradise with Him, and remember the forgiveness and reconciliation that result when He remembers you.

PRAYER

Father, we do not come to your table trusting in our own righteousness. We come trusting in your mercy and the atoning death of your Son.[1] Remember us as we ourselves remember Jesus. Amen.

MORE TO CONSIDER

Do you ever feel like the thief that was crucified by Jesus' side? Would it not have a positive impact on your life to feel that way from time to time, perhaps when taking communion?

---

[1]A rough paraphrase from "The Prayer of Humble Access," in *The Book of Common Prayer* (New York: Church Publishing Inc., 1979), 337.

53

OUR FIRST RESPONSE

WHEN PARTICIPATING in communion, most of us receive bread that we did not bake and juice from grapes we did not grow or squeeze or pour. Most of us receive it from trays we did not prepare, passed to us by other people. More to the point, we receive from it meaning that we could not have generated and a presence of God that we could not conjure up.

- That the bread is in some way the body of Jesus and the fruit of the vine is in some way His blood is not a human idea.

- That He is with us as we participate in the communion is not a human plan.

These truths and realities are not dependent on human emotions or man-made schemes. They come from God, who has revealed Himself to us in Christ as recorded in Scripture.

Our first response to God is always to receive. Just as we received baptism at the hands of another and the meaning and blessing of baptism from the hand of God, we receive communion from the hand of another and the blessing and meaning of communion from God. As the Apostle Paul wrote,

For I received from the Lord what I also passed on to you: the Lord Jesus, on the night he was betrayed, took bread, and when he had given thanks, he broke it and said, "This is my body, which is for you; Do this in remembrance of me." In the same way, after supper he took the cup, saying, "This cup is the new covenant in my blood; do this, whenever you drink it, in remembrance of me." For whenever you eat this bread and drink this cup, you proclaim the Lord's death until he comes.   (1 Cor 11:23-25)

PRAYER

And now, O Lord, we receive gladly that which reminds us of the life and death of Jesus. We open ourselves to the reality of your presence. We thank you for first loving and first giving so that we may learn to love and to give. Amen.

MORE TO CONSIDER

If your first response to God is to receive, what is your second response? How is that evident in your day-to-day life?

54

PUTTING YOURSELF
AHEAD OF GOD

W HEN JESUS INSTITUTED the Lord's Supper, He told the apostles that He himself would be the final Passover Lamb. He took bread and wine and said:

> This is my body given for you; do this in remembrance of me... This cup is the new covenant in my blood, which is poured out for you.
>
> (Luke 22:19-20)

When He spoke those words, they were prophetic. Now they are true and each Sunday, people around the world meet around the Lord's Table to do as He requested.

Because we believe that Communion should be taken reverently and with humility—not with minds racing from one thought to another—our custom is to prepare for communion by focusing our minds on Jesus and His sacrifice. One of the best ways of doing that is to first look inwardly—at our own sinfulness, our own unworthiness.

It is probably not hard to recall a time when you have put yourself ahead of God. Putting yourself ahead of God is what C. S. Lewis called[1] "the basic sin behind all particular sins." "At this very moment," he wrote, "you and I are either committing it, about to commit it, or repenting it."

And so, it is with each of us. As we prepare to take Communion, our attitude should be like the elderly man who stood before his congregation and delivered this simple communion meditation:[2]

> When I was a young man, I thought that when I grew old I would be done with sin. Now as an older man I realize that sin is more powerful to me today than ever before. That is why I need this cup and this bread. That is why I need Communion. That is why I need a Savior, and that is why I am thankful for what my Savior has done.

PRAYER

We have all put ourselves ahead of you on more than one occasion. We cannot come before you this morning trusting in our own righteousness. We come trusting in your mercy and thanking you for the atoning death of Jesus. Amen.

MORE TO CONSIDER

Do you think about your unworthiness before God when participating in the Lord's Supper? Does that unworthiness make you thankful for the grace and mercy of Jesus?

---

[1]C. S. Lewis, *A Year with C.S. Lewis* (New York: HarperCollins, 2003), 104.

[2]Ken Gosnell, "How to give an Effective Lord's Supper Meditation," www.lifeway.com.

55

Examining Yourself

IN 1st Corinthians, the apostle Paul tells us that "Everyone ought to examine themselves before they eat of the bread and drink of the cup" (1 Cor 11:28). And though he does not tell us how to do that, we know from our own experience that the key to conducting a good examination is asking the right questions. So, for example, if you want to test the attitude of your heart before taking the Lord's Supper, ask yourself questions like:

- Is my mindset one of gratitude and humility?

- Am I seeking to grow closer to God?

- Have I confessed my sins lately? Do I intend to?

If you want to know if you are taking the Lord's Supper in a godly manner, with a clear understanding of its nature and purpose, ask some of the obvious questions, like:

- Do the bread and cup remind me of Jesus' broken body and shed blood?

- Do I truly understand the high cost of God's forgiveness?

- Am I holding up my end of the covenant that Jesus died to establish?

Or if you want to know if we as a body commune as Jesus intended, ask questions like:

- Do I help those around me follow Jesus? And do they help me?

- Do I judge people with my mind or with my heart?

- Am I an agent of conflict or reconciliation in the church?

Jesus surely wanted communion to be a time of unparalleled unity among his followers.

Paul saw self-examination as a preventive measure that could help us avoid taking the Lord's Supper in "an unworthy manner" (1 Cor 11:27). And that makes perfect sense because:

- If we do not examine ourselves, we will not recognize our sin.

- If we do not recognize our sins, we will not confess them.

- If we do not confess them, we will not repent of them.

- And if we do not repent of them, we will not be forgiven.

- Without forgiveness, we are separated from God.

- And if separated from God, how can we possibly commune with Him?

So, make it a point to examine yourself.

PRAYER

Father, none of us want to take the Lord's Supper in what Paul called "an unworthy manner." So, help us to examine ourselves in a constructive way, and to approach this solemn time of remembrance with humility and unity and in a way that honors Jesus. Amen.

MORE TO CONSIDER

How many of the questions posed in this meditation go through your mind when taking the Lord's Supper?

56

The Hands of Betrayers

'"WHEN THE HOUR CAME, Jesus and His apostles reclined at the table" (Luke 22:14). According to the Gospel writers, Jesus broke some bread into pieces, gave it to his friends and said, "This is my body..." (Luke 22:19). He took a cup of wine and further explained, "This cup is the new covenant between God and his people—an agreement confirmed with my blood, which is poured out as a sacrifice for you" (Luke 22:20 NLT). At some point in the conversation, He warned the apostles:

> **But the hand of him who is going to betray me is with mine on the table.** (Luke 22:21)

And with the words, "Do this in remembrance of me" (Luke 22:19), He set into motion one of the most important sacraments or practices of the New Testament church—what we call communion or the Lord's Supper.

Now fast forward some 2000 years:

- The hour has once again come.

- The bread and cup are now set before us.

- And we are the disciples who are to remember Jesus—to remember His sacrifice for us and our covenant with God.

Perhaps we should also remember that the hands of betrayers are still at the table, not in the same way that they were when Judas was present, but unless your transformation into a vibrant, mature follower of Jesus Christ is to the point that you no longer sin, you too are bound to betray Him. After all, it was not only Judas who drove Jesus to the cross. It was Adam and Eve, and Abraham and David, a long list of other "good" people, right down to you and me.

So, what are we to do? Exactly what Jesus suggested. Remember the covenant that He died to establish. Continue to trust in it. And if you become discouraged or lose your enthusiasm, know that the way forward is to return to the source that gave rise to your hope in the first place—the atoning blood of God's one and only Son.

PRAYER

The hour is here again, and we know that we continue to fall short of your glory. So, we ask once more for your forgiveness, as we put our trust in Jesus and His redeeming sacrifice on the cross. Amen.

MORE TO CONSIDER

Can you picture yourself as one of the disciples in the upper room? Are your hands clean before Jesus?

57

A COMFORTING MEMORIAL

THERE IS SOMETHING ABOUT Christianity and therefore about communion that is uniquely comforting. After all, it is comforting to remember that Jesus died to make things right between God and us. It is comforting to know that our sins are forgiven and that there is life after death, a place prepared for us in Heaven. But as comforting as that is, it must not be forgotten that our comfort was purchased at a great price. The Psalmist pictured Jesus as a suffering servant and imagined Him saying,

> I looked for sympathy but there was none, for comforters, but I found none. (Ps 69:20-21)

It was not a comfortable sacrifice that Jesus made, and our comfort is in every way dependent on His discomfort.

It should also be remembered that the comfort we receive as Christians does not come because we are seeking comfort, but because we have sought and found truth. As C. S. Lewis once noted, 'In religion, as in war and everything else, comfort is the one thing you cannot get by looking for it. If you look for truth, you may find comfort in the end; if you look for comfort, you will not get either comfort or truth.'[1] The comfort we enjoy as Christians is tied to the truth we have discovered and are remembering this morning about Jesus.

Webster defines a "comfort food" as one that is eaten to maintain a sense of continuity or emotional security, and in that sense, the bread and cup of the communion meal are the ultimate comfort foods. So be comforted when you take the bread and recall the words "This is my body, given for you" (Luke 22:19). Take comfort in the salvation that was secured when the blood of Jesus—like the juice you will be drinking—was "poured out for you" (Luke 22:20).

PRAYER

Dear God, as the apostle Paul once wrote, you are the "Father of compassion and the God of all comfort, who comforts us in all our troubles, so that we can comfort those in any trouble" (2 Cor 1:3-4). Help us to follow the example of Jesus and extend your comfort to those around us. We pray in the name of the one who is our comfort. Amen.

MORE TO CONSIDER

Are you struck by a sense of calm and peace when participating in the Lord's Supper? Do you identify Jesus as the source of that comfort?

---

[1]C. S. Lewis, *Mere Christianity* (New York: Simon & Schuster, 1996), 39.

58

FATHER, SON, HOLY SPIRIT, AND YOU

ONE OF THE AMAZING things we learn as Christians is that God desires a personal relationship with us. It is likely the reason that we were created in God's image. It may be the sole purpose of our existence. It is the reason that as Christians, God inside of us—the Holy Spirit—urges us to seek the Father's presence. It is the reason that God in the flesh—Jesus Christ—died on a cross to reconcile us with His Father. And it explains the fact that when we pray, or study God's word, or take communion, we do so with God's help:[1]

- God is the goal we are trying to reach.

- God is the thing inside of us pushing us toward the goal.

- And God incarnate is the road or bridge over which we can reach the goal.

So, when ordinary Christians like us take the bread and cup of communion, think of them as the body and blood of Jesus, and believe the claim, "This is my body, given for you ... This cup is the new covenant in my blood, which is poured out for you" (Luke 22:19-20), in that moment we are communing with God in three Persons:

- God the Father, who is the object of our desire and whose forgiveness we need.

- God the Holy Spirit, who is working within us, fueling our desire to be reconciled with the Father.

- And God the Son, who laid down His life to atone for our sin and said, "No one comes to the Father except through me" (John 14:6).

Communion, in effect, draws us into a higher kind of relationship—one that God has sought from the moment of creation, and that we were created to be a part of.

PRAYER

God, it is amazing that we can commune with you as Father, Son, and Holy Spirit. You are the goal. You are the motivating force and the path along which we travel. Our job is to be humble and stay out of your way, so that you can complete the work you are doing inside each of us. Help us to do that, I pray in Jesus' name. Amen.

MORE TO CONSIDER

Do you think there is a mysterious interaction involving you, the Father, Son, and Holy Spirit during communion? Might it partially explain your desire to be present when communion is served?

---

[1]C. S. Lewis, *Mere Christianity* (New York: Simon & Schuster, 1996), 153.

59

ASSESSING YOUR LOVE OF GOD

OW MUCH DO YOU LOVE GOD? It is a good question to ask ourselves periodically, because as Paul cautioned the Corinthians in chapter 13 of 1st Corinthians, if you "have a faith that can move mountains," if you give all your "possessions to the poor and surrender" your "body to the flames, but have not love," you "gain nothing" (1 Cor 13:2-3 NIV84).

So, how much do you love God? How do you even measure your love of God? The apostle John gives us two ways:

- "This is love for God:", he writes, "to keep his commands" (1 John 5:3).

- "Anyone who loves God," he adds, "must also love their brother and sister" (1 John 4:21).

In contrast to the feeling-obsessed culture we live in, the Bible reveals that our love of God is not based on subjective feelings that fluctuate over time, but on obeying God's commands and caring for others like we do ourselves. In other words, our actions are the true measure of our love.

In the same way, God's actions are the measure of his love. "How much does God love you?" you might ask:

- 'God demonstrates his own love for us in this:", writes Paul to the Romans, "While we were still sinners, Christ died for us" (Rom 5:8).

- 'This is how God showed his love among us," writes John, 'He sent His one and only Son into the world... as an atoning sacrifice for our sins" (1 John 4:9-10).

God's love, like our love, is a matter of action and of the will.

In the book *The Screwtape Letters,*[1] C. S. Lewis imagines the devil explaining to a young tempter that if they knew what God means by love, the war would be over and they would re-enter Heaven. Fortunately for us, we do know what God means by love. The bread and cup of communion are reminders of God's love, for as the Scriptures make clear, 'Greater love has no one than this, to lay down his life for his friends" (John 15:13).

PRAYER

Father, there is a sense in which to know you is to know love and to reject you is to reject the only kind of love that matters in eternity. Help us each to know you and to love you with all our heart, with all our soul, and with all our mind.[2] And to 'love our neighbor as ourselves" (Matt 22:39). Amen.

MORE TO CONSIDER

Think about how much God loves you and how He demonstrated it. Do your actions reflect a love of God? If not, what can you do to change that?

---

[1]C. S. Lewis, *The Screwtape Letters* (New York: HarperCollins, 2001), 101.
[2]See Matt 22:37.

60

A FRESH START

T HE FIRST day of the year, the first hour of the day, the first day of the week—all are occasions for starting over again. The start of each new day brings fresh opportunities. During a bad day, we have the hope that tomorrow will be better or that after a good night's sleep we will be better able to cope. God created the world with its cycle of days and nights for our benefit. It is a part of God's *common grace* that he not only fine-tuned the universe so that it supports physical human life, but that it is characterized by times and seasons of refreshment and renewal to support man's psychological and spiritual life.

While the new day reflects God's common grace, which is available to all people, the first day of the week has special meaning for Christians. The first day of the week, Sunday, is the day of the week that God raised Jesus from the dead. That is why we worship on Sunday. It is resurrection day. Our belief that God raised Jesus from the dead, and He will raise us as well, gives us great hope for the future and motivation for the present. More than a new day or even a new year, which offer psychological fresh starts, Sunday offers a new start based on a historical reality—the resurrection of Jesus.

But there is a yet more concrete opportunity for Christians to enjoy a fresh start. Jesus provided it in the Lord's Supper, through which we remember His death. His death did something about the past. The best most people can do at the beginning of a new day or week or year is to try to forget the past and intend to do better in the future. During the Lord's Supper, we come as it were into contact with the blood and body of Christ, through which our past is redeemed, and our future is made certain. This newness is always ours, but the Supper reminds us of it in a special way. As Paul wrote to the Corinthians:

> Therefore, if anyone is in Christ, he is a new creation; the old has gone, the new has come! All this is from God, who reconciled us to himself through Christ and gave us the ministry of reconciliation: that God was reconciling the world to himself in Christ, not counting men's sins against them. (2 Cor 5:17)

PRAYER

Lord, there is something in us that longs for a fresh start. We hunger for newness. We gain some satisfaction from the common grace of a new day and a new year, but we thank you and praise you for the real newness that comes from the cleansing that is ours through the sacrifice of your body and the shedding of your blood. We acknowledge your sacrifice for us. We renew our commitment to you and reaffirm our acceptance of our newness as we eat and drink with each other in your Holy presence. Because of Jesus, we pray. Amen.

MORE TO CONSIDER

Do you use the Lord's Supper to begin each week on a positive note, with a fresh awareness of God's love for you?

61

UNITY IN CHRIST

O N THE FIRST SUNDAY of October, Christians around the world, particularly those of the Methodist and Presbyterian traditions, observe what is called *World Communion Sunday*.[1] The goal is to promote Christian unity, which Jesus Himself prayed for in John 17 (John 17:22-23). But not all denominations observe World Communion Sunday, probably because Christians cannot even agree on what Jesus meant when He took the bread of communion and said, "This is my body" (Mark 14:22).

In the March 2022 issue of *Christianity Today*,[2] Dr. James Arcadi outlines some of the ways that those seemingly simple words have been interpreted. They include:

- The bread is miraculously changed into the body of Christ—called *transubstantiation*.

- The bread and Christ's body coexist in the same way that Jesus was both fully human and fully divine—called *impanation*.

- The bread looks and smells and tastes like bread but is changed in a way that is nonetheless real, a way in which Christ's presence becomes known or felt experientially—called *transignification*.

- The bread is merely bread. Christ is present in the same way that He is present anywhere at any time. He is omnipresent.

The Bible does not spell out what Jesus meant by the statement, "This is my body," just as it does not explain what He meant when He said, "My flesh is real food, and my blood is real drink" (John 6:55). Those present on that occasion had to interpret what He meant for themselves. And some responded, "This is a hard teaching" (John 6:60), and no longer followed Him. But the Bible is clear about the meaning and purpose of communion. So, in unity with Christians around the world, we can take the bread and cup of communion at any given time:

- And remember the sacrifice that Jesus made for us on the cross.

- Remember the forgiveness that we receive under the covenant that was consummated by His death.

- And remember the reality that He is with us in Spirit and will one day be with us in resurrected body.

PRAYER

Father, as Jesus desired, may we be one as He is one with you. And may Christians around the world be one so that the world may know that you sent Him and that you love us even as you loved Him.[3] I pray in Jesus' name, Amen.

MORE TO CONSIDER

There are many ways to interpret the statement "This is my body." What do you think it means? Does your view fit within the four that are mentioned here?

---

[1]World Communion Sunday was the brainchild of Dr. Hugh Thompson Kerr, who in 1933 was the pastor of the Shadyside Presbyterian Church in Pittsburgh, PA.

[2]James Arcadi, "'This Is My Body,' Broken into Three Views of Communion," Christianity Today, March 9, 2022, https://www.christianitytoday.com/ct/2022/march-web-only/communion-lords-supper-eucharist-this-is-my-body.html.

[3]See John 17:22-23.

62

Rededication

THERE WAS A TIME when at the end of every worship service at any Christian Church of the Stone-Campbell Movement, a song, like the hymn *Just as I Am, Without One Plea*[1] was played and people were invited to walk down the aisle and profess their faith in Christ or rededicate their lives to Christ. So, whether you were a non-Christian or a Christian, you would hear a weekly call to leave your old self behind and make a fresh start. Although the term "rededicating your life to Christ" is not used in the Bible, that does not mean that the idea is without merit. In fact, it can even make sense within the context of communion. When Paul said,

> **A man ought to examine himself before he eats of the bread and drinks of the cup.** (1 Cor 11:28)

the implication was that if you found yourself lacking, you would at a minimum seek forgiveness, and more than likely redouble your efforts to conform to God's expectations.

In keeping with Paul's warning, confession and absolution precede the Eucharist or Holy Communion in many liturgical worship services. You may just instinctively do those things when preparing to take communion:

- You examine yourself.

- You ask for God's forgiveness.

- And in response to that forgiveness, you humble yourself and resubmit your will to God.

If so, you are rededicating your life to Christ. If not, you might think about doing that when you take the bread and cup of Communion and remember the body and blood of the one who humbled Himself and submitted His will to God for you. And you might pray following the example of David in Psalm 51.

PRAYER

Create in me a clean heart, O God. Renew a right spirit within me. Do not banish me from your presence, and do not take your Holy Spirit from me. Restore to me again the joy of your salvation and make me willing to obey you.[2] I pray in Jesus' name, Amen.

MORE TO CONSIDER

Should people be given an opportunity to profess their faith in Christ at the end of every worship service? Is rededicating your life to Christ something that should be done in public or only in private? When would one or the other make sense?

---

[1]Charlotte Elliott, "Just As I Am, Without One Plea," *Worship and Service Hymnal* (Chicago, IL: Hope Publishing Company, 1957), 198.

[2]See Psalm 51:10-12, NLT.

THE NATURE OF GOD

63   God in the Flesh 155
64   God's Love. 157
65   Love in Action 159
66   God's Forgiving Nature. 161
67   God's Sternness and Kindness. 163
68   Fully God and Fully Man 165
69   The Joy and Faith of God. 167
70   The Humility of God 169
71   A Mindset of Service 171
72   God's Righteousness 173
73   The Grace of God 175
74   God's Grace and Truth 177
75   God Our Father 179
76   What Would Jesus Do?. 181
77   Father Forgive Them 185
78   Remember Me 187
79   Here is Your Son, Here is Your Mother 189
80   My God, My God, Why?. 191
81   I Thirst 193
82   It is Finished 195
83   Into Thy Hands 197
84   Words From the Cross 199

BECAUSE JESUS IS FULLY GOD, the way He handles the events leading up to His crucifixion, as well as the crucifixion itself, reveals a great deal about God's character. The meditations in this section explore what Jesus' behavior tells us about the nature of God. The first meditation, *The Most Important Verse*, introduces the idea that Jesus reveals God. The remaining meditations address some of God's most important attributes—His love, humility, commitment to justice, grace, and so on. Meditations 77-84 are focused on what the words of Jesus from the cross reveal about God's nature. Additionally, *Married to Christ* in the final section of the book[1] addresses the love of God.

---

[1]Meditation 95.

63

GOD IN THE FLESH

W HEN A PERSON PROMINENT in his field identifies something in that field as the most important, it should capture your attention and curiosity. For example, when E. Stanley Jones, missionary and prolific Christian writer, said in one of his books that this is the most important verse in scripture, you should take note, and when a few pages later, he quotes renowned New Testament scholar William Barclay saying, "it might well be held that this is the greatest verse in the whole New Testament," it should really grab your attention. The verse to which Jones and Barclay were referring is John 1:14:

> The word became flesh and made his dwelling among us. We have seen his glory, the glory of the one and only Son, who came from the Father, full of grace and truth. (John 1:14)

The word became flesh. Those are remarkable words, but words have limitations. If we think of the word God, we think of the highest meaning of God to us, but the *meaning of God* is not God. It is our best understanding of God. If we think of love, we are really thinking of our best understanding of love, but that is not love. It is our best understanding of the word love. If we think of sacrifice, we think of our best understanding of sacrifice, but our best understanding of sacrifice is not sacrifice, it is only our best understanding of the word. The same could be said of grace and truth.

In order to reveal Himself to us, God did not send us words. He sent us the word made flesh. If we want to see the love of God or His sacrifice, we look to the word made flesh among us. The baby Jesus was not an idea but a real baby, the man Jesus, who taught and performed miracles and was crucified, was actual flesh and blood. The body on the cross was real, and the one raised from the dead with wounds into which Thomas thrust his fingers was flesh. The word became flesh and dwelt among us.

When we remember Him, as we do during the Lord's Supper, it is not with candles lit because He was the light of the world. It is not with incense burned as the sweet fragrance rises heavenward. It is not with the soft sounds of bells ringing. It is with the firm sometimes crunchy unleavened bread and the cool grape flavored liquid in the cup prepared by faithful servants, distributed by fellow believers, held in our hands and taken into our mouths. We remember that it was not a dream or a phantom or an idea or ideal that we honor here. It is someone corporal and real. It is the word become flesh who dwelt among us full of grace and truth.

PRAYER

Our Father, we thank you that you have not revealed yourself to us in words, but in the word made flesh. We pray that by your spirit the word will become flesh again in us as we take the life of Christ into our lives in the loaf and the cup, the body and the blood. Amen.

MORE TO CONSIDER

Is it difficult for you to think of God as a man? Can you think of the ways He suffered as a man on the cross? Can you imagine the ways He suffered as God on the cross?

64

GOD'S LOVE

According to John chapter 13:

> It was just before the Passover Feast. Jesus knew that the time had come for him to leave this world and go to the Father. Having loved his own who were in the world, he now showed them the full extent of his love. The evening meal was being served and the devil had already prompted Judas Iscariot, son of Simon, to betray Jesus. Jesus knew that the Father had put all things under his power, and that he had come from God and was returning to God; so he got up from the meal, took off his outer clothing, and wrapped a towel around his waist. After that, he poured water into a basin and began to wash his disciples' feet . . . (John 13:1-5)

It was not the sort of thing that we would do, facing death by crucifixion and knowing that all things were under our power. That kind of power opens a lot of tempting alternatives to washing feet and dying on a cross. And history suggests—both God's record and our own—that we are not very good at resisting temptation. But Jesus was. He knew where He had come from and where He was going. And He was determined to show the world the full extent of His love.

Less than a day after washing the disciples' feet, Jesus hung on a cross, and people were shouting:

> He saved others ... but he can't save himself!　　(Matt 27:42)

> Come down from the cross if you are the Son of God!　(Matt 27:40)

They were emboldened by His lack of power, because Jesus did not respond with power. He responded with love:

> This is my body, given for you . . . my blood, which is poured out for you.　　　　　　　　　　　　　　　　　(Luke 22:19)

He willingly took our sin upon Himself and endured the punishment we deserve. He showed both the world and us the full extent of God's love.

Prayer

We thank you for Jesus and His love—so pure that it cannot be corrupted by power, so forgiving that it can save us from our sin, and so unconditional that it is available to us all. May we, like Jesus, demonstrate it to others through our own lives. Amen.

More to Consider

Is there any greater proof of God's love than the sacrificial death of His Son on the cross? Does anything about His sacrifice motivate you to sacrifice for Him?

65

LOVE IN ACTION

ONE OF THE CHALLENGES of living between earth and Heaven is that it is not always easy to separate fact from fiction. For example, when people say they love God but behave as though they do not, do they really love God or do their actions speak louder than their words? Jesus talked about the importance of both words and actions on several occasions,[1] including in a parable where a father asks his two sons to work in a vineyard. One son is quick to say that he will, but then does not follow through. The other son flatly refuses to work, but later changes his mind and does. Jesus asked the simple question, 'Which of the two did what his father wanted?" (Matt 21:31) Clearly, both sons' actions spoke louder than their words.

In the context of the Bible's claim that 'God is love" (1 John 4:8, 4:16), Jesus is the action that speaks louder than the words. Sacrifice, after all—giving up something of value for the sake of someone else—is the most reliable measure we have of love. So, Jesus's sacrifice on the cross is the most persuasive proof we have of God's love. The writers of the New Testament knew that. Think about:

God so loved the world that He gave his one and only Son. (John 3:16)

God demonstrates His own love for us in this: While we were still sinners, Christ died for us. (Rom 5:8)

> This is love: not that we loved God but that he loved us and sent his
> Son as an atoning sacrifice for our sins.   (1 John 4:10)

All those scriptures and Jesus's own words, "This is my body given for you
... my blood, which is poured out for you" (Luke 22:19-20), are lived out
on the cross.

- When you look at a cup of communion, you should see the blood
  of Jesus.

- When you look at the bread of communion, you should see His
  broken body.

- When you look at either, you should see God's love.

"God is love" (1 John 4:8, 4:16) and Jesus is God's love in action.

Prayer

Father, thank you for your love. And we pray that as we journey between
earth and Heaven, we will share that love with those around us in both
word and deed. Amen.

More to Consider

God expressed His love for us in both words and deeds. Does His example
convince you that words alone cannot equally express our love for
humanity?

---

[1]See Luke 6:46, Matt 7:21-22.

66

GOD'S FORGIVING NATURE

HERE IS A PETITION in the Model Prayer that Jesus gave us that is a little surprising:

And forgive us our debts, as we also have forgiven our debtors, [*goes the prayer. Jesus explains it by adding,*] For if you forgive other people when they sin against you, your heavenly Father will also forgive you. But if you do not forgive others their sins, your Father will not forgive your sins.   (Matt 6:12, 14-15)

This seeming linkage between God's behavior and our behavior is frightening. Many commentators observe that God's forgiveness is conditional. If we do not forgive, He does not forgive. That seems to contradict what we think we know about grace and works. It is a sort of a negative way to understand the petition. On this side of the cross, a better way to understand the passage might be this. Those believers who fully understand the forgiveness of God will necessarily be characterized by forgiveness themselves. If I understood that God took away all my sin because of His love for me, how can I not forgive those comparatively tiny offenses against me.

We sometimes see Christians respond to a major offense with a forgiving attitude, like the black Christian man who hugged and forgave the white police officer who mistakenly killed his brother.[1] Or the members of the Charleston, SC church who forgave the white man who went to their church, took part in their prayer meeting, and shot and killed nine members of the church.[2] That would be hard. But most of us do not find ourselves in that kind of situation. Most refuse to forgive our neighbors for some little selfish and petty thing, and in some cases, we may not even remember what our neighbor did to offend us, but we nevertheless continue with an unforgiving spirit.

The way of the serious Christian is to forgive others as a way of life, because God has forgiven them. Jesus lived a life like that, a life characterized by forgiving sins. While in the process of bearing the sin of the world, He said of those who had any part in His death,

> **Father, forgive them; for they do not know what they are doing.**
> (Luke 23:34)

And not being one of those who could forgive mankind in general but not people specifically, He said to the thief who hung next to Him,

> **Today you will be with me in paradise.** (Luke 23:43)

In other words, you are forgiven. Among other things, the Lord's Supper reminds us of His forgiveness and motivates us to live lives characterized by forgiveness.

PRAYER

We pray, Our Father, that in light of your gracious forgiveness, you will heal us of our selfishness and pettiness and inspire us by your great sacrificial love as we drink the cup and eat the bread of forgiveness. Amen.

MORE TO CONSIDER

Is there someone in your life that you need to forgive?

---

[1]"Man honored for hugging Amber Guyger, COP who killed his brother Botham Jean in his own apartment," 6abc.com, December 4, 2019, https://6abc.com/amp/amber-guyger-hug-botham-jean-brandt/5733281/.

[2]Luke Barr and Alexander Mallin, "DOJ reaches settlements with victims' families in 2015 Charleston church shooting," abcNEWS, October 28, 2021, https://abcnews.go.com/amp/Politics/doj-reaches-settlements-victims-families-2015-charlestonchurch/story?id=80835815.

67

GOD'S
STERNNESS AND KINDNESS

THINK FOR A MOMENT about the sternness and kindness of God.[1] That is what the apostle Paul asked the Christians of Rome to do in Romans chapter 11. And any reasonable view of God must account for both His sternness and His kindness. They are not mutually exclusive.

So, if you think of God as only kind, like a doting father or a tolerant friend, remember the cross and Jesus' body and blood. They are a powerful reminder that God must be true to Himself, no matter what the cost:

- Because of His righteousness, He is forced to judge our unrighteousness.[2]

- Because of His holiness, He is forced to judge unholiness.

- And because of His purity, He is forced to judge impurity.

Even if it means the crucifixion of His only Son.

But if you think of God as only stern, like an angry judge, remember again the cross and Jesus' body and blood. For on the cross, God—through the sacrifice of Jesus—is revealed:

- Not as vindictive.

- Not as one to whom justice is the only thing that matters.

- But as a God who is willing to take the consequences of our sin upon Himself.

The ultimate expression of God's kindness, the covenant of grace, was forged on the cross.

So, as you take the bread and the cup, consider this: The cross puts both the sternness and the kindness of God on display. We would be wise to remember both.

PRAYER

We thank you that because of Jesus' death on the cross, you are somehow able to separate us from our sin. You can exercise both sternness and kindness in a way that preserves justice and extends mercy to all who will receive it. Grant us your mercy. Amen.

MORE TO CONSIDER

Some believe that we develop our image of God from our earthly fathers. Does that seem to be true for you? Was your earthly father primarily stern or kind? Does that prevent you from reconciling both aspects (i.e., His sternness and kindness) of God's character?

---

[1]See Rom 11:22.

[2]See Bob Martin, *God Our Father* (Johnson University Press, 2011), 43.

68

FULLY GOD AND FULLY MAN

ONTROVERSIES IN the earliest centuries of the church forced church leaders to define the nature or essence of Christ. Though other terms were used, the one that has lasted for more than 1700 years and is accepted in nearly all branches of the church is that Jesus was *fully God and fully man.* One nature, fully God, plus one nature, fully man, equals one *Jesus nature.* If that does not add up, it is because any God who is small enough for us to get our heads around is not big enough to be God.

That the word became flesh and dwelt among us focuses on the reality that Jesus was fully man and accepts the truth that Jesus was fully God. John made the belief that Jesus was man a test of faith when he wrote, "This is how you can recognize the Spirit of God: Every spirit that acknowledges that Jesus Christ has come in the flesh is from God" (1 John 4:2). Here are some of the characteristics of Jesus' human nature that we see in the Bible:

- He was born of a woman (Luke 2:7). He grew in the normal way, increasing in wisdom and stature (Luke 2:40, 52).

- He was tempted (Luke 4:1-13).

- He experienced tiredness (John 4:6), thirst (John 19:28), hunger (Matt 4:2), weakness (Matt 4:11, Luke 23:26), and pain (the cross).

- He had human emotions. He was amazed in His heart (Matt 8:10); He was sorrowful (John 11:33-35); He wept (John 11:35); His soul was troubled (John 13:21).

- His knowledge could be limited. When asked about the second coming, He acknowledged that He did not know the day or hour (Mark 13:23)

- He had a will of his own. He said He did not do His will, but the will of the Father (John 6:38). He prayed in the garden, not my will but yours (Matt 26:39).

He was, as the writer of Hebrews affirms, "fully human in every way" (Heb 2:17), but there was a way in which he was different— "he did not sin" (Heb 4:15), and the Hebrew writer gives a reason for this. It was "so that he might make atonement for the sins of the people" (Heb 2:17). The final thing that Jesus did in His full humanity was to die. To be fully human, human like us, He had to die, and because He died without sinning, He could atone for the sin of humanity.

PRAYER

Our Father, the juice and the bread remind us of the blood and the body of the one who was fully man, the one who was also fully God, the one you exalted to the highest place and gave the name that is above every name. We eat the bread with thanksgiving for His obedience, and we raise our cup with great hope for our eternity. We always pray in His name. Amen.

MORE TO CONSIDER

Considering the ways in which Jesus demonstrated His humanity, it is amazing that He was able to live without sin. Because He was fully God, He was raised from the dead, showing us what will happen when we die with our sins forgiven. Read Philippians 2:5-9 to learn more about the attitude of Christ and, incidentally, the nature of God.

69

THE
JOY AND FAITH
OF GOD

HEBREWS 12:2 offers us as Christ followers some sound advice—advice that is particularly relevant when preparing to take the Lord's Supper:

Let us fix our eyes upon Jesus, the author and perfecter of our faith, who for the joy set before him endured the cross... (Heb 12:2 NIV84)

Some have suggested that the writer of Hebrews uses the name Jesus instead of Christ in this passage to encourage us to look at Him as a man—so that we would focus on His humanity.[1] After all, it was through His humanity that He became the author and perfecter of faith:

- His entire earthly existence revolved around trusting God.

- He showed us what "living by faith" looks like in human form.

- And when instituting the Lord's Supper, He directed our attention to His Humanity. "This is my body," He said, "given for you... my blood," He added, "which is poured out for you" (Luke 22:19-20).

It would be easy to argue that it was faith that enabled Jesus the man to endure the cross, and it no doubt played an important role. But the author of Hebrews claims that it was "the joy set before him" that made the real difference. What was the joy? It surely was not the pain of crucifixion or disappointment of being rejected by those He was trying to save. The joy must have been:

- His imminent reunion with the Father.

- The honor and glory of that reunion, having all things put under Him.

- And bringing those that He loved to salvation—making us part of the joy.

So, recognizing that you are a part of his joy:

> Let us fix our eyes upon Jesus, the author and perfecter of our faith, who for the joy set before him endured the cross, enduring its shame, and sat down at the right hand of the throne of God.
>
> (Heb 12:2 NIV84)

PRAYER

Father, we are grateful for the faith of Jesus and want to be more like Him in our own faith. We thank you for the joy that enabled Him to endure the cross on our behalf and we fix our gaze upon Him this morning, determined to remain a part of His joy. Amen.

MORE TO CONSIDER

Jesus trusted God and demonstrated a faith that has since to be reproduced. God also trusted His Son to become *fully human* without falling victim to sin. How faithful are you? With respect to God's joy, have you ever thought of yourself as part of the joy that, according to the writer of Hebrews, enabled Jesus to endure the cross? Are you living a life that makes His joy complete?

---

[1] R. Kent Hughes, *Hebrews: An Anchor for the Soul* (Wheaton: Crossway Books, 2015), 385.

70

THE
HUMILITY
OF GOD

I N THE FIRST OF TWO known letters to his young assistant, Timothy, the Apostle Paul included these words:

> Here is a trustworthy saying that deserves full acceptance: Christ Jesus came into the world to save sinners—of whom I am the worst.
> (1 Tim 1:15)

It is one of five "trustworthy sayings" found in Paul's writings. And like the other four, it contains a key teaching that we all believe is true—in this case, that Jesus came into the world to save us. But unlike the others, this saying ends on a personal note—a confession of sorts—that when you stop to think about it, is probably something we all sometimes feel as well. For when we come to the communion table and think about the life and death of Jesus, we cannot help but see that in the light of His goodness we are the worst of sinners too. Whether we compare His sinless life to our good intentions, or His forgiving nature to our impatience with others, or His sacrificial death to our tendency to put ourselves first, we look bad because we are.

No matter how you look at it, remembering Jesus is a humbling experience. Even when it comes to humility; He also set the standard for that. Paul points this out in a letter to the Philippians:

> Your attitude should be the same as that of Christ Jesus: Who, being in very nature God, did not consider equality with God something to be grasped. But made himself nothing, taking the very nature of a servant, being made in human likeness. And being found in appearance as a man, he humbled himself and became obedient to death—even death on a cross. (Phil 2:5-8 NIV84)

PRAYER

We thank you that even though we are the worst of sinners, Jesus came into the world, humbled Himself, and gave His life to save us. His body was broken; His blood was shed. And we know that it is only because of Him that we can say, just like Paul did to Timothy: "But for that very reason I was shown mercy so that in me, the worst of sinners, Christ Jesus might display his unlimited patience as an example for those who would believe on him and receive eternal life" (1 Tim 1:16). Amen.

MORE TO CONSIDER

Some have said that you cannot be a real Christian until you realize that you are a real sinner. Paul obviously realized that, and it changed the trajectory of his life. Has it done the same for you?

71

A MINDSET OF SERVICE

SUBMISSION is not an easy topic for arrogant self-seeking 21st Century Americans, not even for arrogant, self-seeking 21st Century American Christians. However, no great leader asks of his followers what he will not do himself. Consider what Paul says about Jesus in Philippians 2:5-11. He might have been quoting an early Christian hymn.

> In your relationships with one another, have the same mindset as Christ Jesus: Who, being in very nature God, did not consider equality with God something to be used to his own advantage; rather, he made himself nothing by taking the very nature of a servant, being made in human likeness. And being found in appearance as a man, he humbled himself by becoming obedient to death, even death on a cross!
>
> (Phil 2:5-11)

This passage brings at least four pictures to mind:

1. Jesus added to Himself the *nature of a servant*. Think of Jesus in the upper room at the Last Supper washing the feet of His apostles and urging them to live with the same mindset. He was God taking on the nature of a servant.

2. Jesus was by all appearances a man. We do not know what Jesus

looked like, but picture a man hungry and thirsty, or weary, or aggrieved, or angry. Picture a man born and reared among men and working a trade. He was by all appearances a man. But He was God incarnate, God appearing as a man, God fully man.

3. Jesus humbled Himself and obeyed God. Picture Him praying in the Garden of Gethsemane, first asking for His own will to be done, then submitting to God in a prayer that we could all recite, "Not my will but yours be done" (Luke 22:42). He was the Son submitting to the Father.

4. And finally, Jesus was crucified. Picture Jesus dying on a cross. It is not an image we want to hold long in our minds. He was the man-God who died on a cross.

It is this sort of humility, selflessness, and service to others that we are to imitate and that we are reminded of in the Lord's Supper. Then Paul tells the rest of the story.

> **Therefore God exalted him to the highest place and gave him the name that is above every name, that at the name of Jesus every knee should bow, in heaven and on earth and under the earth, and every tongue acknowledge that Jesus Christ is Lord, to the glory of God the Father.** (Phil 2:9-11)

PRAYER

Our Father, we are reminded in this communion service that if we are to be like Christ, we will be like Him in humility and obedience. Help us then, as we remember Him, to do nothing out of selfish ambition or vain conceit, rather, in humility to value others above ourselves, not looking to our own interests but each to the interests of the others. Amen.

MORE TO CONSIDER

It is one thing to be humble. It is another to be selfless and obedient. And it is yet another to behave as a servant of others. Jesus did them all and we are the beneficiaries of His service. In what ways do you serve those around you?

72

GOD'S RIGHTEOUSNESS

FOR THIRTY-SOMETHING YEARS, Jesus was a lot like us. He cried when his good friend, Lazarus, died.[1] He got angry when merchants used the temple of God for their own gain.[2] He had parents, siblings, and friends like us; somehow earned a living like us. And remember this prayer: "Father, if you are willing, take this cup from me" (Luke 22:42). It seems that just like us, not all His prayers were answered in the way He would have preferred. One of the most basic tenets of the Christian faith is that God's Son became like us. According to Hebrews 2:17, it was necessary for Jesus to be in every aspect like us, His brothers and sisters.[3]

Though Jesus became like us, there is a big difference between being like us and behaving like us. And though Jesus surely understands our weaknesses, for He faced all the same temptations we do, unlike us, He did not sin.[4] And that makes Him worthy of our attention. There is something about being like us and being without sin that is valued by God:

- Had Jesus come to earth and behaved like us, there would be no perfect sacrifice to wash away our sin.

- Had He stayed in Heaven, outside of our world and beyond the agony of the cross, no amount of righteousness could make up for what we have done.

- Only after becoming like us and living without sin, could the death of God's Son have the power to save. Only then could it give us the covenant of grace.

So, on the eve of His crucifixion, because He was like us, Jesus was able to say, "This is my body, given for you" (Luke 22:19). And because He was without sin, He was able to add:

> "This cup is the *new covenant* in my blood, which is poured out for you" (Luke 22:20).

PRAYER

We are grateful for the sinless life that Jesus lived and for the sacrifice that He made on the cross, for it surely took the life and death of one who was without sin to save us all from our own sin. Forgive us because of what He did. Amen.

MORE TO CONSIDER

One important nature of God is that He never changes. Another is that He cannot sin. Because Jesus demonstrated the latter during his life on earth, we can trust Him to fulfill the promises recorded in the Bible. Why do you think that it was not possible for Jesus to save us without becoming a man?

---

[1]See John 11:35.

[2]See John 2:15-16.

[3]See Heb 2:17.

[4]See Heb 4:15.

73

THE GRACE OF GOD

From the fullness of his grace we have all received one blessing after another. For the law was given through Moses; grace and truth came through Jesus Christ.　　　　　　　　　　　　(John 1:16-17 NIV84)

THINK FOR A MOMENT about grace, about the one who brought grace into your life, and how His body and blood, the focus of communion, made that possible:

- The grace of God was made possible by a selfless, one-of-a-kind sacrifice. It took the blood of a man who had faced our temptations without making our mistakes.

- God's grace was contingent on a brutal punishment—a body stretched out on a cross, suffocating under its own weight. A life separated from the source of life, forever wounded, for you and for me.

- And because life as God designed it is "an affair of the will,"[1] the grace of God required a man with the willpower to obey God unconditionally.

It took a man who would choose to resist temptation and freely accept the punishment we deserve. When we participate in the Lord's Supper, we are reminded that the only man who could do all that was more than man—He was God's incarnate Son.

In the 2007 film, *As Seen Through These Eyes*,[2] twelve Holocaust survivors are questioned about their experiences in Nazi death camps. And near the end of the film, one of the survivors recalls praying this, "Oh God, don't forgive them... for they know what they're doing." He could not imagine extending grace to the soldiers who had tortured him and taken the lives of his family and friends. But while securing God's grace for us, Jesus prayed from the cross, "Father, forgive them, for they do not know what they are doing" (Lk 23:34).

No wonder we remember His broken body and shed blood. He, in essence, suffered "death by sin"[3] so that we could have life by grace.

Prayer

Father, may we never forget that it is by grace that we have been saved, through faith— "and this not from ourselves, it is a gift of God" (Eph 2:8). Thank you for the grace that we have through the sacrificed body and blood of your Son. Amen.

More to Consider

Grace is easy to receive, but hard to give. Do you think those who sin against you know what they are doing from an eternal perspective? Does the Lord's Supper teach you the importance of extending grace to the ungracious?

---

[1] C. S. Lewis, *A Year with C.S. Lewis* (New York: HarperCollins Publishing, 2003), 280.

[2] *As Seen Through These Eyes*, directed by Hilary Helstein (Parkchester Pictures, 2007).

[3] E. B. Filler, *Effective Meditations for the Offering and Communion* (Lincoln, NE: Writers Club Press, 2000), 55.

74

GOD'S GRACE AND TRUTH

The Word became flesh and made his dwelling among us. We have seen his glory, the glory of the one and only Son, who came from the Father, full of grace and truth... For the law was given through Moses; grace and truth came through Jesus Christ. No one has ever seen God, but the one and only Son, who is himself God and is in closest relationship with the Father, has made him known. (John 1:14-18)

THESE ARE POWERFUL words about God from the first chapter of John. God became flesh in Jesus. If you want to see God, look at Jesus through whom God has made Himself known. When we think about the Lord's Supper, we see at least two characteristics of God that are uniquely revealed in Jesus—grace and truth. John writes: "We have seen his glory, the glory of the one and only Son, who came from the Father, full of *grace and truth*" (John 1:14). He reaffirms it by noting that "*grace and truth* came through Jesus Christ" (John 1:17). Grace and truth are two glorious characteristics of God that Jesus shows us. They are important and belong together:

- Truth alone can be hard and cold like a nail. It can be rough like a splinter filled timber. Truth can be sharp like a thorn or the point of a spear. It can sting like a whip.

- Grace alone can be a loving behavior or a forgiving attitude. It can be warm and gentle like a welcome or an affirming word. It can be smooth and soothing like a smile, like the touch of a helping hand.

Truth balances grace. Grace softens truth. But Jesus brought them together. Truth and grace are mingled on Golgotha's brow. There, the open wounds of a flogged back pressed against the splinters of an old, rugged timber. A man pinned by cold hard spikes, wearing a crown of thorns, dies.

- Truth is the reality of the awfulness of sin and the necessity of punishment.

- Grace is the man-God Jesus choosing to hang there, speaking forgiveness for His enemies, accepting the sinner beside Him, caring for His mother, suffering unspeakable physical pain, crying out in spiritual anguish, dying for us.

During the Lord's Supper, we are confronted by and remember all of this.

> While they were eating, Jesus took bread, and when he had given thanks, he broke it and gave it to his disciples, saying, "Take and eat; this is my body." Then he took a cup, and when he had given thanks, he gave it to them, saying, "Drink from it, all of you. This is my blood of the covenant, which is poured out for many for the forgiveness of sins." (Matt 26:26-28)

PRAYER

Thank you, Lord, for the truth of the Gospel, and thank you for the grace of our Lord Jesus Christ. In the juice and the bread and in the presence of fellow believers, we remember both your grace and your truth. Amen.

MORE TO CONSIDER

What would our fallen world be like if God were characterized by truth alone? How would it look if He were defined by grace alone? Do you see why we should thank God for both?

75

GOD OUR FATHER

S EVERAL NAMES are applied to God in both the Old and New Testaments. Most of them refer to one or another of His wonderful characteristics—His majesty, might, authority, superiority, or royalty, for instance. However, when Jesus comes to reveal God most fully and finally, He refers to Him most frequently by the name "*Father.*"

- He is sent from the Father and will return to the Father, He says.[1]

- "Our Father in heaven" (Matt 6:9), He teaches us to pray.

- He claims to speak the words of the Father and does everything the Father sent Him to do.[2] God is His Father and He is a perfect Son.

- He loves the Father. Once, in a seemingly emotional outburst, He proclaims, "I praise you, Father" (Luke 10:21).

And He taught us that we could be adopted children of the Father and enjoy His provision and protection and share in His inheritance.

At the same time, there is something unreasonable and unfair about the fatherhood of God that must not go unnoticed. In order to restore a rebellious world, He had, as the Scripture says, "to give his only begotten Son" (John 3:16), not to lend Him, but to give Him. Most fathers would not entertain the idea of allowing their sons to be killed for the benefit of others. Fathers can rationalize themselves out of that situation, but God so loved the world that He gave.

So, it is not the power or majesty or any of the attributes that are reflected in the myriad names for God that most distinguishes Him as a Father; it is His love. At immeasurable cost, He purchased our salvation through the death of His only Son, Jesus, on a cross.

PRAYER

Our Father, we come to you as children because we depend on you for life. We want to share in the inheritance of Jesus and enjoy your provision and protection. And we recognize that Jesus is the means by which that is possible. We thank you that He lived the life of an obedient Son and sacrificed Himself so that we could be adopted into your heavenly family. Amen.

MORE TO CONSIDER

Except for His prayer on the cross, Jesus always prayed to God as Father. Have you considered the implications of Jesus teaching us to also address God as 'our Father'?

---

[1]See John 14:13.
[2]See John 14:10.

76

WHAT WOULD JESUS DO?

I N 1896, CHARLES SHELDON published the book *In His Steps: What Would Jesus Do?*[1] A hundred years later, youth leader Janie Tinklenberg[2] read the book and began putting the acronym WWJD on bracelets to remind teens to always ask themselves the question: What would Jesus do? It is a good question. We should all ask ourselves that question from time to time, but there is a more important question to consider when preparing for the Lord's Supper: What did Jesus do?

The New Testament, of course, answers that question, and gives us several well-written summaries of what Jesus did, summaries that are believed to have been used as early Christian creeds. They are concise statements of the shared beliefs of the first Christians; statements that were in use before the New Testament was even written. Some of them are indented in your Bible to set them apart from the rest of scripture. In 1st Timothy, for example, Paul records this one:

> He appeared in the flesh, was vindicated by the spirit, was seen by angels, was preached among the nations, was believed on in the world, was taken up in glory. (1 Tim 3:16)

In Philippians, he records another—this one focused on the nature and attitude of Jesus:

> Who, being in very nature God, did not consider equality with God
> something to be used to his own advantage; rather, he made himself
> nothing by taking the very nature of a servant, being made in human
> likeness. And being found in appearance as a man, he humbled himself
> by becoming obedient to death—even death on a cross! (Phil 2:5-11)

And in 1st Corinthians, Paul documents yet another, and claims that it is
of "first importance":

> That Christ died for our sins according to the Scriptures, that he was
> buried, that he was raised on the third day according to the Scriptures,
> and that he appeared to Cephas, and then to the Twelve. After that,
> he appeared to more than five hundred.   (1 Cor 15:3-6)

When instituting the Lord's Supper, Jesus also directed our attention
to that which is of first importance—His atoning death on the cross. The
most important thing that that accomplished was to reconnect us with
God—what the New Testament calls reconciliation. Considering all that
Jesus did, the appropriate response is three words that some consider to
be one of the earliest Christian creeds. They are found in Romans 10,
where it is noted:

> If you declare with your mouth, "Jesus is Lord," and believe in your
> heart that God raised him from the dead, you will be saved.
>
>   (Rom 10:9)

Communion is good time to confess, "Jesus is Lord."

Prayer

Father, at the end of John's gospel, he noted that the whole world would
not have room for the books that could be written about all that Jesus
did.[3] It is impossible for us to know and understand all that He did, but we
can grasp enough to recognize that Jesus is Lord. And we proclaim that
this morning as we take the bread and cup in remembrance of His body
and blood and all that He did for us. Amen.

MORE TO CONSIDER

If your church has its roots in the Stone-Campbell Restoration Movement, how do you square the ideas expressed above with the movement's slogan, *No creed but Christ, no book but the Bible*? If not, does your church use creeds in their weekly worship services? What is their purpose? Do you feel that they add to your understanding of scripture?

---

[1]Charles Sheldon, *In His Steps: What Would Jesus Do* (1896).

[2]"What would Jesus do?" Wikipedia, last modified July 20, 2023, https://en.wikipedia.org/wiki/What_would_Jesus_do%3F.

[3]See John 21:25.

77

FATHER FORGIVE THEM

THE FIRST WORDS that Jesus spoke from the cross were words of forgiveness: "Father, forgive them for they do not know what they are doing." He was right, of course. The soldiers did not know what they were doing. They were obeying their orders. They were doing their duty. The religious leaders, Annas, Caiaphas, and the Pharisees did not know what they were doing. They thought they were carrying out their religious responsibilities. They had convinced themselves that they were doing God's work. The political leaders, Herod and Pilate, did not know what they were doing. They were simply doing what political leaders do. They were doing what was expedient, what would advance their personal agendas. The crowd certainly did not know what they were doing. None of them knew that they were killing the Son of God.

The truth is all humanity was included in the prayer of Jesus. "He came to that which was his own, but his own did not receive him" (John 1:11). Sadly, the words of Jesus include us as well. The old hymn asks, "Were You There When They Crucified My Lord?"[1] and our answer is yes. We did not pound in the nails, but our sin put Him on the cross. Whenever we sin, our sin adds to His pain and suffering. He died for all sinners and for all sin. To the extent that we do not understand that reality, we do not know what we are doing. Whenever we pray for forgiveness, we are praying for more suffering for Jesus, because that is how our forgiveness comes. Our dilemma is that there is no other way to obtain forgiveness.

The only consolation is that we know He wants us to be forgiven. That is why He died on the cross.

Communion gives us the opportunity to remember what we did to Him and what He does for us.

PRAYER

Our Father, we confess this morning that so much of what we do is characterized by ignorance. We understand too little of your holiness and the seriousness of sin and the meaning of forgiveness and the cost of redemption. Even so, we eat the bread and drink the cup and we try to remember, and we try to understand, and we thank you. Amen.

MORE TO CONSIDER

Did you ever consider that in the mystery of God's time and foreknowledge your sins add to the suffering of Jesus on the cross? If you were conscious of that, that is, if you knew what you were doing, would it change your response to temptation?

---

[1] *Were You There?*, Traditional Spiritual. *The Hymnal for Worship and Celebration.* Word Music, Waco, 1986, 181.

78

Remember Me

The soldiers also came up and mocked him. They offered him wine vinegar and said, "If you are the king of the Jews, save yourself." There was a written notice above him, which read: this is the king of the Jews. One of the criminals who hung there hurled insults at him: "Aren't you the Messiah? Save yourself and us!" But the other criminal rebuked him. "Don't you fear God," he said, "since you are under the same sentence? We are punished justly, for we are getting what our deeds deserve. But this man has done nothing wrong." Then he said, "Jesus, remember me when you come into your kingdom." Jesus answered him, "Truly I tell you, today you will be with me in paradise."

(Luke 23:36-43)

THE ROMANS HUNG JESUS BETWEEN TWO THIEVES. In the image of prophecy, He was numbered among the transgressors.[1] They did this to humiliate Him, but it did not work. These were His kind of people. Often seen with sinners, He had been to parties with publicans and conversed with questionable women in public. When criticized, He said that it was not the healthy who needed a doctor, but the sick.[2] He said that He came into the world to seek and save the lost.[3] If they had asked Him where He wanted to be crucified, He might have answered, "Over there, between those two criminals."

They had hung a sign on the cross that said, "King of the Jews." One of the thieves denounced Him saying, "If you are the king of the Jews, save yourself and us." It was another insult in a long line of insults. The other thief said, "This man has done nothing wrong." "Jesus," he said [*he was the only person in the Bible to address Jesus simply as Jesus, rather than Jesus son of David or some other title*] remember me when you come into your kingdom." Jesus answered, "Today you will be with me in paradise." That was enough.

- He is what makes paradise, paradise.

- He is what makes heaven, heaven.

- To be with Him is life's greatest hope and heaven's greatest promise.

When you come to the Lord's Table, you are that thief, guilty of sin, deserving of death, crying out "Jesus," hearing Him answer, "Today you will be with me."

PRAYER

Lord, we remember you as people who were condemned to death because of our sins. In our desperation, we called on you and you remembered us, and so in the bread and the fruit of the vine, we remember you and thank you. Amen.

MORE TO CONSIDER

What do you think persuaded one thief to conclude that Jesus had done nothing wrong? Did you ever consider identifying with the thieves as you participate in communion? Do you see how it could enrich your experience?

---

[1]See Isa 53:12.

[2]See Matt 9:12.

[3]See Luke 19:10.

79

HERE IS YOUR SON,
HERE IS YOUR MOTHER

Near the cross of Jesus stood his mother, his mother's sister, Mary the wife of Clopas, and Mary Magdalene. When Jesus saw his mother there, and the disciple whom he loved standing nearby, he said to her, "Woman, here is your son," and to the disciple, "Here is your mother." From that time on, this disciple took her into his home.

(John 19:25-27)

THE LORD'S SUPPER is about the death of Jesus, and the gospels record many of His dying words. The words, "Father forgive them for they do not know what they are doing" (Luke 23:34), are words of *mercy* or *forgiveness*. His remark to the thief beside Him, "Today you will be with me in paradise" (Luke 23:43), are words of *hope*.

Among the people at the foot of the cross were His mother and the apostle John. He said to His mother, "Woman, here is your son," referring to John. To John, He said, "Here is your mother" (John 19:26-27). These are words of *love*, for in them He provided for their earthly needs to love and be loved in His physical absence.

Mary loved Jesus as only a mother loves, and her heart was indescribably broken at His crucifixion. In John's account of the Lord's Supper, he

189

speaks of the "disciple whom Jesus loved," who was "reclining next to him" (John 13:23). It was John. He and his brother James had once been called the *sons of thunder*, but in response to the embrace of Jesus, John became the *apostle of love*. "My little children, you ought to love one another," became one of his favorite sayings.[1]

A wedding ring, a golden heart, a diamond, are for many symbols of a love that lasts forever. However, the greatest symbol of everlasting love is the old rugged cross. But the thing Jesus gave us to remember the cross was not the cross, but the cup and the loaf. A cross is a symbol, but the cup and the loaf continue in some inexplicable way to be real. Some of the things that we remember about Jesus at the Lord's Table are the mercy, hope, and love that Jesus taught us.

PRAYER

Lord, thank you for the love that you showed to us by your death on the cross and which we remember today in the cup, which is your blood, and the loaf, which is your body. In eating and drinking them may we become so filled with your love that we become more loving. Amen.

MORE TO CONSIDER

Three of the seven statements that Jesus made from the cross are noted above. What were the other four and what do we learn about God's nature, if anything, from them? The accounts are found in Matthew 27, Mark 15, Luke 23, and John 19.

---

[1]Toward the end of John's life, he is said to have summed up the entire message of Christ in this one sentence and repeated it over and over again.

80

MY GOD, MY GOD, WHY?

They went to a place called Gethsemane, and Jesus said to his disciples, "Sit here while I pray." He took Peter, James and John along with him, and he began to be deeply distressed and troubled. "My soul is overwhelmed with sorrow to the point of death," he said to them. "Stay here and keep watch." Going a little farther, he fell to the ground and prayed that if possible the hour might pass from him. "Abba, Father," he said, "everything is possible for you. Take this cup from me. Yet not what I will, but what you will."   (Mark 14:32-36)

THE WORST EXPERIENCE Jesus had was on the cross. But it was not the humiliation of being crucified, the skull piercing crown of thorns that was placed on His head or falling under the weight of its splintery beams while carrying it to the site of His execution. Nor was it the penetration of the thick dull nails that fastened Him to the cross, the crushing agony of it being dropped into a hole, or even the helplessness of hanging upon it with no hope of rescue. It was not His separation from family and friends that Jesus dreaded most. It was the thing that brought Him to His knees in the Garden of Gethsemane as He pleaded with God for another way.

If it was pain and suffering that Jesus feared, or even physical death, we must admit that others have faced it as bravely. When Jesus cried out,

"My God, My God, why have you forsaken me?" (Mark 15:34) He revealed the thing that He greatly feared. The one who had always known God, who had been with Him from the beginning, would for the first time in Divine history be without God. He would experience the hell it is to be without God. In an incomprehensible way, God would be divided from Himself. We imagine Jesus in heaven with the scars on His hands and feet and side, but that is only a small part of the reality. God Himself is forever scarred. This was the only way to bridge the gulf between the holiness of God and sinfulness of man, and Jesus was willing to do it. God was willing to do it. This price that Jesus paid for our salvation is one of the things we remember around the Lord's table.

PRAYER

Our Father, we cannot begin to understand the price you paid on the cross or the depth of your love that caused you to do it. Sometimes all we can say is thank you. We can only observe the communion with awe and gratitude. Amen.

MORE TO CONSIDER

The process of dying can be scary, but the most frightening thing is death without God. Are you giving as much attention to protecting your soul as you are to taking care of your body?

81

I Thirst

Jesus said to them, "Very truly I tell you, it is not Moses who has given you the bread from heaven, but it is my Father who gives you the true bread from heaven. For the bread of God is the bread that comes down from heaven and gives life to the world." "Sir," they said, "always give us this bread." Then Jesus declared, "I am the bread of life. Whoever comes to me will never go hungry, and whoever believes in me will never be thirsty." (John 6:32-35)

JESUS EXPERIENCED temptation, hunger, thirst, anger, sadness, pain, and bleeding. However, nothing in the life and ministry of Jesus expressed His humanity more than the word translated, "I thirst," (John 19:28) spoken from the cross. The cross was a great spiritual battle that Jesus had dreaded and prayed in the garden to avoid if there were another way. There was not. Hanging on the cross, He asked God to forgive His crucifiers. He forgave the thief at His side and arranged for His mother's care. As the spiritual battle deepened, He cried out to God who had indeed forsaken Him for the sake of humanity. Alone, the spiritual battle over, a hurting, bleeding human, he moaned "I thirst." It was hard. He had refused the first drink offered to Him. There was no certainty that anyone would respond. In this cry, He identified not only with humanity, but with needy humanity. He identified with us. He was one with us.

But if the cross reminds us that He could be thirsty, it also assures us that He was the answer to thirst. To the woman at the well (John 4), He had said, "whoever drinks the water I give them will never thirst." He clarified that on a different occasion when He said, "whoever believes in me will never be thirsty" (John 6:35). On that day, He also referred to Himself as the "bread of life." While the bread we eat during communion may not satisfy a physical hunger and the juice may not quench a physical thirst, our participation will certainly energize our spirits and sustain our souls.

PRAYER

Our Father, we believe that Jesus was fully human and experienced all the kinds of things that we experience. We thank you for His willingness to suffer as He did. We also believe that He was fully divine and did for us what we could never do for ourselves. Most importantly, He died on the cross as a substitute for us. We remember those things with thanksgiving whenever we observe the Lord's Supper. Amen.

MORE TO CONSIDER

Jesus showed His humanity, not only by being thirsty on the cross, but by admitting His thirst. Does His willingness to admit His weakness encourage you to be open about your needs both to God and to your fellows?

82

IT IS FINISHED

N JOHN 19, as His life is about to end, Jesus makes this simple yet profound statement:

"It is finished." (John 19:30)

"With that," according to John, "he bowed his head and gave up his spirit" (John 19:30).

Some have suggested that those three words eclipse all the other words ever spoken by Jesus. They come from a single Greek word that can be translated "it is completed" and that conveys the general idea of a goal achieved or result attained. Despite appearances, though dying on a Roman cross, Jesus maintains that He is accomplishing what He came to earth to do, what He sometimes called the work the Father had given Him. That work was motivated by the fact that God cannot forgive us for our sin based on His love for us alone. His forgiveness and our reconciliation with Him are contingent upon the atoning death of His Son.

God did not have to create a world in which we could sin. But having done so, He felt it necessary to send His Son to die for our sin, for there was no other way for God to be who He is—that is, to be true to Himself—and make creation what He wants. So as Jesus gave up His spirit, completing the work the Father had given Him, it was appropriate for Him to say, "It is finished." There was no need to wait until the resurrection. The work had been done, restitution had been made, the justice demanded by God's holiness was served, and sin and death were defeated. The resurrection was the Good News because it validated what Jesus asked us to remember around the Lord's Table and then affirmed on the cross: "It is finished" (John 19:30), I have paid your debt in full, you are forgiven.

PRAYER

Father, it is finished. And the bread and cup of communion are powerful reminders of how it ended—with Jesus' broken and bleeding body suspended on a cross, doing for us what we could not do for ourselves. We thank you again for His unselfish sacrifice and the amazing grace that it made possible. Amen.

MORE TO CONSIDER

What does this statement from the cross say about Jesus' mindset as He was about to die? What might you have said with your dying breath?

83

INTO THY HANDS

G OD SENT JESUS into this world with a mission as indicated in that well-known passage recorded in John 3:16. To carry out that mission, Jesus lived the life that God intended. "The Son can do nothing by himself; he can only do what he sees the Father doing" (John 5:19), He proclaimed. He completed His mission on the cross in a demonstration of sacrificial love beyond human comprehension. The first three sayings from the cross were words of love and forgiveness: "Father, forgive them, for they do not know what they are doing" (Luke 23:34), "today, you will be with me in paradise" (Luke 23:43), "woman, here is your son, here is your mother" (John 19:26-27). The fourth was a cry of agony, "My God, my God, why have you forsaken me" (Mark 15:34). That tragic experience expressed in these words was all a part of the divine plan. His next words, "I thirst," (John 19:28) demonstrated His humanity. Then He declared His mission accomplished, "It is finished" (John 19:30). And finally, He said, "Father, into your hands I commit my spirit" (Luke 23:46). With His human life over, the one who trusted God from the beginning, yielded His spirit back to God.

For Jesus, life had always been about trusting God. He never stopped trusting God, even when circumstances required that God turn His back on Him. God had a plan for His life, and He knew it and He followed it to the end. God has a plan for our lives, too. His plan is that we faithfully follow Jesus. The communion service is a regular reminder of Jesus on the cross, asking God to forgive us, suffering for our sins, and finally yielding Himself back to God. Because of Him, we are forgiven people committed to following Him until the day we commend our own spirits to God.

PRAYER

Our Father, nothing seems more central to the meaning of the communion service than the cross. And yet, Jesus told us that the great meaning of the cross is expressed not in that age-old symbol, but in the loaf and the cup, representing His body and blood. They speak to us of the deep meaning of the cross. We will long remember what was said there, and as we eat and drink, we shall never forget what He did. It is with solemn memories and deep gratitude that we participate in the communion. Amen.

MORE TO CONSIDER

How do you understand the common expression that God has a plan for your life? Do you understand it to describe His goal for you to follow Jesus, or do you understand it to be a specific detail design for every step of your life? How are you responding to your understanding of God's plan?

84

WORDS FROM THE CROSS

After taking the cup, he gave thanks and said, "Take this and divide it among you. For I tell you I will not drink again of the fruit of the vine until the kingdom of God comes." And he took bread, gave thanks and broke it, and gave it to them saying, "This is my body given for you; do this in remembrance of me." (Luke 22:17-19)

I

T WAS ONLY HOURS after Jesus had spoken the words instituting the Lord's Supper in the upper room that He spoke the *words from the cross*. What are commonly called the seven words are seven sentences or seven sayings. In the Greek it is 41 words; in the NIV translation it is 51 words. They are spaced out over the six or seven hours that Jesus was on the cross—the first three clustered toward the beginning and the last four at the end. You can find some of the words in each of the Gospels, but you must read at least three of them to get all of them. Here they are in their probable order:

Father forgive them for they do not know what they are doing.
(Luke 23:34)

I tell you the truth, today you will be with me in paradise.
(Luke 23:43)

Here is your son . . . Here is your mother.	(John 19:26-27)
Eloi, Eloi, Lama Sabachthani.	(Matt 27:45)
I am thirsty.	(John 19:28)
It is finished.	(John 19:30)
Father, into your hands I commit my spirit.	(Luke 23:46)

Here they are by theme:

- The first two statements are about the reason for the cross. If He wanted to "forgive those who did not know what they were doing" (Luke 23:34), this was the only way. If He wanted to promise paradise to the thief, this was the only way. Someone had to die for the sin of the world, either the sinner or the Savior.

- The third word, "Here is your son . . . Here is your mother" is the word He spoke to the disciple John about His mother, Mary. He was setting His affairs in order before the inevitable. He would rise from the dead, but He would also ascend into heaven, so with Joseph apparently dead, someone would have to care for Mary. John took her in.

- The middle statement is the word of despair. It is the "why" question that we all ask on occasion. My God, my God, WHY? It was the cup that He submitted to in the Garden of Gethsemane when He prayed "Not my will but your will be done."

- The last three words demonstrate, first, His humanity— "I am thirsty." He knew what it was to suffer. Second, His victory, "It is finished"—not I am finished, but the work I was sent to do, the work that caused me to cry out "My God, my God, why have you forsaken me"—that work is finished. And finally, He spoke the word of trust despite everything: "Into your hands, I commit my spirit."

When we participate in communion, it is good to remember His words from the cross.

PRAYER

Our Father, as we taste the bread and sip the juice, we are reminded of your death, that you tasted fully and the cup that you drained completely. The words you spoke from the cross guide our thoughts as we remember. We are thankful for your love and forgiveness, and we repent of our sins and the unimaginable agony they caused you. We praise you for what you accomplished on the cross and we recommit ourselves to you as we eat and drink and remember. Amen.

MORE TO CONSIDER

The seven statements that Jesus made from the cross tell us a lot about Jesus and consequently about God's nature. If you have only those seven statements to draw from, what would your impression of God be? How would you describe God?

THE HUMAN
PREDICAMENT

85   Worldview 205
86   Reality. 207
87   Culture Wars. 209
88   Understanding Scripture 211
89   The Problem With Individualism 213
90   Some Common Heresies. 215
91   Finding the One Way to God 217
92   Closed Membership and Open Communion 219
93   Self-Centeredness 221

THE HUMAN PREDICAMENT is that we have all disobeyed God
and have no way to rectify the situation of our own accord.
The natural tendencies of man—e.g., our proclivity to sin—
affect the way we behave and understand God. The meditations in this
section address man's tendencies or characteristics as they relate to our
understanding and acceptance of the sacrificial death of Jesus on the cross.
The subjects covered are relevant to today's culture and range from our
individualism to our culture and worldview.

85

WORLDVIEW

Your worldview is the lens through which you see life. It is the understanding through which you make sense of experience. The simplest and clearest expression of the Christian worldview can be summarized in three short sentences.

FIRST: The world is good. When God created the world, He saw that it was good, very good. To list all the goodness of creation would be impossible:

- The gentle breeze of a perfect summer day
- The beauty and wonder of a limitless starlit sky
- The love of a mother
- Great art and music as the creature imitates the creator
- A kidney donated to a stranger
- Acts of sacrifice, service, and kindness
- Feelings of joy
- A sense of satisfaction

There is enough goodness in the world to make an atheist ask, *"If there is not God, why is there so much goodness in the world?"*

SECOND: The world is fallen. The sinfulness of man has brought God's curse on the world:

- The air and skies are polluted
- The love of a mother is aborted
- Pornography is called art and dissonance is called music
- Prisoners are killed for their body parts
- Selfishness, exploitation, and violence are common
- Feelings of despair abound
- A sense of hopelessness is pervasive

There is enough evil in the world to make a Christian ask, *"If there is a God, why is there so much evil?"*

THIRD: The world is being restored. From Noah to Abraham to Moses to the Prophets to Jesus to the Church, God has engaged in a plan to completely restore goodness and root out the vestiges of evil. The fulfillment of the plan was in His Son Jesus, who died for the sin of the world and commissioned His followers to spread the good news to all the world, making disciples of all nations. Paul urged Christians to take every thought captive for Christ's sake. To the extent that we are faithful, we participate in the restoration of good.

There is no better reminder of our Christian worldview than the Lord's Supper. Here we remember the perfect man, who lived a life of love and light, met a fallen world and was killed, and whose death was made the instrument of the world's salvation.

The world is good. The world is fallen. The world is being restored.

PRAYER

Father, the world is being restored. You turned an evil act of a fallen world into good, and we thank you for Jesus, who makes our restoration possible. Amen.

MORE TO CONSIDER

What is your worldview? Does it in any way differ from the Christian worldview as presented above?

86

REALITY

I N THE BOOK *Total Truth,*[1] Nancy Pearcey points out a flaw in thinking common to our culture and not uncommon to church members. Others before her, including C.S. Lewis and Francis Schaeffer, have recognized the same flaw. The flaw involves dividing reality into two categories. A common image is a two-story house in which some aspects of experience reside on the first story and some on the second story. In this case, science, reason, and facts are on the lower floor and religion, faith, and values are on the second. The lower story information is of public value; the upper is of private value.

This is how a scientist or biology teacher can work all week as though there is no God and worship Him on Sunday. She is operating on the lower story during the week and the upper story on Sunday. This is how a politician can believe life begins at conception but vote for abortion. One view is his personal and private second story view; the other is his public and reasonable lower story view. This is also how two opposite religious teachings can be viewed as not being contradictory. In the sphere of values facts do not matter.

The thinking that separates reality into the public and private, religious and scientific, facts and values is wrong. The truths that we celebrate in the Lord's Supper—the life, death, resurrection and living presence of Jesus—are not upper story values; they are hard facts. Jesus, Himself, is the central unifying truth of history, reason, and fact, as well as religion, faith, and values. He is the way, the truth and the life.

> For I received from the Lord what I also passed on to you: the Lord
> Jesus, on the night he was betrayed, took bread, and when he had
> given thanks, he broke it and said, "This is my body, which is for you;
> Do this in remembrance of me." In the same way, after supper he took
> the cup, saying, "This cup is the new covenant in my blood; do this,
> whenever you drink it, in remembrance of me." For whenever you eat
> this bread and drink this cup, you proclaim the Lord's death until he
> comes. (1 Cor 11:23-26)

PRAYER

Lord, we remember in this communion Jesus, who came in history, took
on human form, lived among us, loved us, taught truth, was killed on the
cross, raised from the dead, ascended to the Father, and lives by His spirit
among us today. Bless the bread and the juice as they remind us of His
reality then and now. Amen.

MORE TO CONSIDER

Do you live as though reality is divided into two separate categories? Can
you see the fallacy of living with that sort of attitude?

---

[1]Nancy Pearcey, *Total Truth: Liberating Christianity from its Cultural Captivity*
(Wheaton: Crossway Books, 2004), 20-22.

87

CULTURE WARS

I N THE BOOK *Soul Survivor*,[1] Philip Yancey recounts interviewing writer Annie Dillard for the magazine *Christianity Today*. Annie is a gifted nature writer who, at the time, weaved her faith in God into her books. She won the Pulitzer Prize for her book *Pilgrim at Tinker Creek* at the age of 22. In her interview with Yancey, she noted her fascination with the Old Testament account in Kings where Josiah orders the temple to be cleaned and discovers the Law. She was flabbergasted. How could a nation that was rescued from Egypt have forgotten God? How could they have misplaced the book of the law? How does a nation forget God, she wondered.

Dillard's question is not so hard for us today. We are living it. For Israel, it was hundreds of years of neglect and the competition of seemingly more attractive gods. For us, it is the enemies of God aggressively attempting to eliminate God and particularly Christ from all aspects of human experience. The American Civil Liberties Union, Americans United for the Separation of Church and State, the Foundation for Freedom from Religion, and Black Lives Matter are but a few of the noble sounding organizations that want to purge America of her religious heritage.

Today, Christianity is being removed from our schools at an alarming rate—prayer and moments of silence intended for prayer, devotions for athletic teams, the mention of Jesus in student commencement speeches, and the reading of the Bible. And it is not only our schools but also the public square as well, where the Ten Commandments and nativity scenes are no longer welcome and Supreme Court candidates are considered suspect if they are too religious. We live in a nation that has forgotten or at best is forgetting God.

How can a nation that is forgetting God or has forgotten God, remember God? The first step is certainly for the church to remember God, and one good way is through the faithful observance of the Lord's Supper. But it is not enough to simply remember God as the dispenser of forgiveness and grace. Christians must faithfully represent God in the home, the school, the workplace, the public square and the voting booth. We must boldly represent Him in the spoken word, in our overall behavior, and in the written word.

Annie Dillard had a unique way of looking at things. She asked not only how a nation can forget God, but how can a nation remember God. Sadly, she now lists her religion as "none" on her web page. Her journey is not over, but she has taken a serious turn. Her powerful influence has been muted. We must remember God and represent Him well. In a post-Christian world, we must be faithful to the end.

PRAYER

Our Father, as we witness what seems to be the loss of the cultural war, let us never forget who you are and who we are. The bread and juice of communion remind us of what you did for us and what we must do for you. You died bravely and humbly for us. May we live both graciously and boldly for you. Amen.

MORE TO CONSIDER

Are you openly expressing your faith when the situation calls for it and subtly expressing it in every situation? Do you vote for candidates whose policies are in harmony with Scripture? What else do you do?

---

[1]Philip Yancey, *Soul Survivor* (Colorado Springs: Doubleday, 2001), 227.

88

Understanding
Scripture

AT ONE POINT IN THE PAST, preaching was interpreting the Shakespearian English of the *King James Bible* and explaining how words change over time. Today, people start with a Bible they can understand, and the preacher is left with the daunting task of explaining what the passage may have meant to the original reader and what it means to today's believer. We must infer what the inspired writer meant for us to take away from the passage. Some passages seem to be culturally bound, like the role of women in the church, while others have application to both the original reader and us.

Very few passages speak clearly and unequivocally to or about you and me today. However, at least two do just that. The first is after the resurrection of Jesus. He had already appeared to many of the apostles, but Thomas, having not been present, says:

> "Unless I see the nail marks in his hands and put my finger where the nails were, and put my hand into his side, I will not believe." A week later his disciples were in the house again, and Thomas was with them. Though the doors were locked, Jesus came and stood among them and said, "Peace be with you!" Then he said to Thomas, "Put your finger here; see my hands. Reach out your hand and put it into my side. Stop doubting and believe." Thomas said to him, "My Lord and

my God!" Then Jesus told him, "Because you have seen me, you have believed; blessed are those who have not seen and yet have believed."

(John 20:24-29)

We are among those who have not seen and yet have believed. As such, we have received the favorable words of Jesus—blessed are those.

The second passage is also from John. It is the prayer of Jesus in the upper room before His death:

My prayer is not for them alone. I pray also for those who will believe in me through their message, that all of them may be one, Father, just as you are in me and I am in you. May they also be in us so that the world may believe that you have sent me. (John 17:20-22)

We are the ones for whom Jesus prayed.

These two passages offer great truths that are reflected in the Lord's Supper. It is here that we proclaim our confidence in that which we have not seen with our own eyes. We take the things that we can see and touch and taste and smell, the bread and the juice, and we use them to remind ourselves of the thing that we did not see and yet believe with all our hearts—that Jesus died, was buried, was raised from the dead, and lives forever. And we simultaneously demonstrate our unity by participating with local believers and millions of believers worldwide, uniting with them on the one thing about which we can all agree—Jesus.

PRAYER

Our Father, we regret the seeming disunity of the church, but we participate in the Lord's Supper in solidarity this morning with the millions across the globe and across time who are indeed united by your spirit. We thank you for the gracious blessing you pronounced on those of us who by faith have believed what we did not see. We express that faith in our communion this morning. Amen.

MORE TO CONSIDER

As you participate in the Lord's Supper on any given Sunday, do you have a sense of unity with all Christians, everywhere, at all times and places?

89

The Problem with Individualism

J AMES EMORY WHITE, the preacher of a megachurch in North Carolina, once found himself in a dilemma over communion. His church used the internet to broadcast their regular worship services to shut-ins, the sick, and those who were traveling. They also provided chat rooms where people could talk to church leaders and developed a vibrant online congregation of people who participated only through the internet. The church normally celebrated communion on Wednesday evenings but decided to move the service to their weekend worship. Wanting their internet congregation to participate, what would they do about communion? Would they tell that group to go to the kitchen and get some juice and bread? It was a problem.

The problem is uniquely American and contemporary. It is caused by our emphasis on *individualism.* It is not a by-product of technology, for the idea of taking communion alone has probably been considered by many in church history—by a prisoner, for example, or a person confined to their home.

The thrust of the Bible and the sense of the church is that communion is something one does in community. That is, communion is not only communion with God, but with each other. It is the way we renew our baptismal commitment to God and to each other. It is the way we express unity with each other. It is the way we proclaim the Lord's death to each other. We take the bread and juice from a common tray. We are served by servers who are our brothers in Christ, and we pass the loaf and cup to serve each other. There are no socio-economic, class or racial distinctions at the Lord's Table. We are family. It is communion in community.

Luke writes in Acts: "On the first day of the week, we came together to break bread" (Acts 20:7). It was the practice of the early church and the primary purpose of the assembly. In 1 Corinthians, Paul writes that the Corinthian Church had developed a habit of having a love feast as a part of their Lord's Day celebration, and that it had deteriorated to the point that they hardly made a distinction between that feast (*intended to feed their bodies*) and communion (*intended to feed their souls*). It was also characterized by class distinctions. So, he told them that if the rich and the poor could not eat in a loving way, they should eat the meals at home, but not the Lord's Supper. He gave them these instructions:

> For I received from the Lord what I also passed on to you: the Lord Jesus, on the night he was betrayed, took bread, and when he had given thanks, he broke it and said, "This is my body, which is for you; Do this in remembrance of me." In the same way, after supper he took the cup, saying, "This cup is the new covenant in my blood; do this, whenever you drink it, in remembrance of me." For whenever you eat this bread and drink this cup, you proclaim the Lord's death until he comes. (1 Cor 11:23-26)

PRAYER

Our Father, we thank you for the fellowship that we have together and that we can share in communion with you. Bless the loaf and the cup and thank you for the sacrifice that made it possible and meaningful. Amen.

MORE TO CONSIDER

Have you ever taken communion alone, perhaps during the pandemic of 2020? Did it feel awkward or make you wish that you were participating with others?

90

SOME COMMON HERESIES

IN THE BOOK *Bad Religion,* New York Times columnist Ross Douthat contends that we have become a nation of heretics. He mentions four ways in which we are heretical:[1]

1. The first is *liberal Christianity's constant effort to redefine the Biblical Jesus.* We get a regular diet of headlines about new gospels that are nothing more than ancient heresies reborn. They want a Jesus who fits the times or who calls historical Christianity into question.

2. Another heresy is the *pray and grow rich cult,* currently epitomized by Texas preacher Joel Osteen, but foreshadowed by some powerful positive thinkers and possibility thinkers of the past. For them, the purpose of Jesus is the comfort and convenience of the believer.

3. A third heresy is the *spiritual but not religious movement* that finds god everywhere, most notably in you. It is a religion in which you are god. It is the triumph of feeling over belief. That is, it does not matter what you believe, so long as you feel good about yourself.

4. The fourth heresy that Douthat sees in America today is the heresy of *nationalism or mixing religion and politics* in such a way that they are inseparable.

The answer to these heresies can be found at the Lord's Table:

1. Who is the real Jesus? The one who died for us and asked us to remember His death through communion.

2. What is the place of riches in our lives?

    Whoever wants to be my disciple must deny themselves and take up their cross and follow me. (Luke 9:23)

    But seek first his Kingdom and his righteousness and all these things will be given to you as well. (Matt 6:33)

3. In the battle between feeling and belief, Jesus points us, at the Lord's Table, to the facts that we believe—He is God, we are not, and He died for us in space and time.

4. As for the mixing of religion and politics, conservative Christians may have much in common with a political party, but at the Lord's Table we renew our commitment to our God, who we recognize as the highest authority in our lives.

PRAYER

Our Father, we are thankful that you have given us the communion which constantly reminds us of the source and direction of our faith and sets for us the priorities of our lives. Be with us as we remember that which is of greatest importance to us. In Jesus name, Amen.

MORE TO CONSIDER

Are any of the heresies mentioned above of relevance to your life? Have you known people who have fallen for any of them?

---

[1]Ross Douthat, *Bad Religion* (New York: Free Press, 2012).

91

FINDING THE
ONE WAY TO GOD

IMAGINE YOURSELF ON A JOURNEY aboard a ship. A terrible storm appears, and the ship is battered for 14 days. You cast everything overboard in order to save lives. Finally, fearing the ship is going to crash into the rocky shoreline and sink, you decide it is every man for himself, and you secretly prepare to launch the ship's only lifeboat to save yourself.

But one man, who claims to be speaking for God, warns against it. You know him to be a person of unusual insight and who seems to be in touch with God. He predicted the storm; now he predicts salvation to those who stay on board. So, you cast your lot with him. You cut the lifeboat loose and remain on board. If he is right, you are saved. If you are wrong about him, all is lost.

A story like this is, in a sense, a parable of life. We are all on the journey of life. We all face the storms of life. Confronted at some point with a word from God, we are forced to accept it and cast our lot with it or reject it. In other words, we go out on our own and try to save ourselves or stay with those on the ship and trust the word from God.

We stay. We believe. Jesus is the only way.

Christians are often criticized for believing that Jesus, who is that word from God, is the only way to God. Critics complain about what this seems to say about the beliefs of others, but it constrains our options as well. When we say that Jesus is the only way, we are also limiting our own choices. We have made our decision. We have gotten on board with Christ. We acknowledge no other options for ourselves. He is the truth and the only truth about reality. He is the only source of life, now and forever. His way is the only way to follow. No matter how bad the storm or how dim our prospects of survival seem to be, we will stay with Him. We agree with the one who said, "Though he slay me, yet will I hope in him" (Job 13:15).

We reaffirm this when we participate in the communion. Our trust for time and eternity, in fair seas and foul, is in the one who died for us, who lives in us, and who has gone to prepare a place for us.

PRAYER

Our Father, you and we have no "plan B." With the loaf and the cup, we remember your death for us, your life in us, and your promise to us. In doing so, we reaffirm our trust in you and you alone. Amen.

MORE TO CONSIDER

How do you justify to others that Christianity is the only way to salvation? Have you ever thought about telling them that it restricts your options as well?

92

CLOSED MEMBERSHIP AND OPEN COMMUNION

I T HAS BEEN more than 100 years since the official break between the Christian Churches and the Non-instrumental Churches of Christ. There are many on both sides who would like to see reconciliation between the two groups. Both the Independent Christian Churches and the Non-instrumental Churches of Christ, as well as the Disciples of Christ denomination, grew out of a church unity movement dating back to the early 1800's and known as the Restoration Movement.

The Restoration Movement had as its goal restoring to the church certain New Testament teachings and emphases that had been lost over the years. It was not meant to create a denomination but a movement within the larger church. Two of the biblical teachings that it sought to restore to their original meaning were baptism and the Lord's Supper.

The emphasis on baptism and the Lord's Supper reflects the spirit and genius of the Restoration Movement and is a characteristic of the churches that practice *closed membership* and *open communion* today. What does that mean? On the day of Pentecost, convicted sinners cried out "What must we do to be saved?" (Acts 2:37) And Peter answered:

Repent and be baptized in the name of Jesus Christ for the remission of sins and you will receive the gift of the Holy Spirit. (Acts 2:38)

Churches of the Restoration Movement have taken this to be the normative Biblical answer to the question. Baptism in the New Testament was immersion in water, so they have understood baptism to be the immersion of a repentant believer in water for the remission of sins and the gift of the Holy Spirit. Baptism is not a work but an act of faith. It is not something you do, but something that is done to you.

Only a few years after the break between the instrumental and non-instrumental fellowship of believers another break was looming with the group that became the Disciples of Christ denomination. One of the issues was the practice of some missionaries and churches to accept people into membership who had not been immersed—called *open membership.* Churches that practice *closed membership* accept into their congregations only those who have surrendered to Christ in what is understood to be biblical baptism. Closed membership says that they take seriously what they understand to be the teaching of the New Testament.

Now you would think that a church that practiced closed membership would also practice *closed communion,* but that is not necessarily the case. Some churches require you to be a member of their church—or to prove that you are a Christian—to take communion; others do not. At the Lord's Table, however, the invitation to communion comes from Him. The Lord's Supper is for all believers who consider themselves to be children of His. *Open communion* says that, despite strong convictions on the answer to the question about how to be saved, in the final analysis your relationship with God is between you and the Lord.

PRAYER

Lord, we are committed to the unity of all believers and understand the church, as Jesus envisioned it, to be non-denominational in nature and built upon His atoning sacrifice on the cross. We thank you for that in Jesus' name. Amen.

MORE TO CONSIDER

Does your church practice open communion? Is its membership closed? How do you interpret the scriptures mentioned above?

93

SELF-CENTEREDNESS

O N THE DAY AFTER Jesus miraculously fed a crowd of 5,000, many followed Him to the other side of the Sea of Galilee, where He taught them the meaning of that event. In His message, He looked back to the time that God provided manna from heaven during the wilderness wandering. He told them that believing and obeying Him is food for their souls. And unknown to them, He looked forward to the Lord's Supper. His words, spoken about a year before the Lord's Supper was instituted, could have been spoken that very night:

> When they found him on the other side of the lake, they asked him, "Rabbi, when did you get here?" Jesus answered, "Very truly I tell you, you are looking for me, not because you saw the signs I performed but because you ate the loaves and had your fill. Do not work for food that spoils, but for food that endures to eternal life, which the Son of Man will give you. For on him God the Father has placed his seal of approval." Then they asked him, "What must we do to do the works God requires?" Jesus answered, "The work of God is this: to believe in the one he has sent." So they asked him, "What sign then will you give that we may see it and believe you? What will you do? Our ancestors ate the manna in the wilderness; as it is written: 'He gave them bread from heaven to eat.'" Jesus said to them, "Very truly I tell you, it is not Moses who has given you the bread from heaven, but it is my Father who gives you the true bread from heaven. For the bread of God is the

bread that comes down from heaven and gives life to the world."
(John 6:25-33)

Continuing,

Jesus said to them, "Very truly I tell you, unless you eat the flesh of
the Son of Man and drink his blood, you have no life in you. Whoever
eats my flesh and drinks my blood has eternal life, and I will raise them
up at the last day. For my flesh is real food and my blood is real drink.
Whoever eats my flesh and drinks my blood remains in me, and I in
them. Just as the living Father sent me and I live because of the Father,
so the one who feeds on me will live because of me. This is the bread
that came down from heaven. Your ancestors ate manna and died, but
whoever feeds on this bread will live forever."   (John 6:53-58)

As a result of these words, the people were confused, the religious
leaders were offended, and the disciples were puzzled. They did not see
that the figures of eating His flesh and drinking His blood were figures for
taking Him into our lives, like eating food that both strengthens us and
becomes a part of us. At the upcoming Passover, Jesus would teach His
followers to act out the eating of His flesh and drinking of His blood, which,
because of His death on the cross, would have even greater meaning.

There is a verse in these passages that is a bit surprising. Jesus
criticizes the crowd by saying, 'I tell you the truth, you are looking for me
not because you saw miraculous signs, but because you ate the loaves and
had your fill" (John 6:26). This seems odd, because He seems to be saying
that they should have been following Him because of His miracles. But
that is exactly right. The miracles point to Jesus and who He is. That is
why He performed them. The miracles focus our attention on Him. But
this was not so with the crowd. Their question was, 'What is in it for me?
What can I get from the miracles?" Jesus had fed the 5,000 one time, and
they wanted manna every day, like that provided by God through Moses
in Old Testament times. Their focus was wrong.

About a year later:

While they were eating, Jesus took bread, and when he had given
thanks, he broke it and gave it to his disciples, saying, "Take and eat;

this is my body." Then he took a cup, and when he had given thanks, he gave it to them, saying, "Drink from it, all of you. This is my blood of the covenant, which is poured out for many for the forgiveness of sins."   (Matt 26:26-28)

The right question for us—the thing to remember—is not just what the death of Jesus means for me, but rather what the death of Jesus says about Jesus.

PRAYER

Lord, thank you for what the death of Jesus says about Jesus. Thank you for His love, His pain, and His sacrifice. Thank you for Him. Bless the loaf and the cup as we stop thinking about ourselves and focus on that which is excellent and praiseworthy, the one who is true, noble, right, pure, lovely, and in every way admirable. Amen.

MORE TO CONSIDER

Our natural inclination as humans is to focus on our own welfare. When participating in the Lord's Supper, are you able to focus on the one who died to make your salvation possible?

SPECIAL OCCASIONS

94   A Rescue Mission. 227
95   Married to Christ. 231
96   Our Hope and Peace 233
97   What Child Is This? 235
98   The Adoration of the Christ Child. 239
99   Christmas 243
100 Easter 245
101 Thanksgiving. 247
102 New Year's Day 249
103 Independence Day 251
104 Communion for Children 253

THERE ARE OCCASIONS, like Christmas and Easter, when a meditation for the Lord's Supper can be informed by the occasion itself. There are also times when the meditation should be directed to a particular audience, like children. The meditations in this section address some of those occasions. *Married to Christ*, for instance, could be used at a wedding. Additionally, *God Our Father*[1] from the section entitled *The Nature of God* would be an appropriate meditation on Father's Day.

---

[1]Meditation 75.

94

A RESCUE MISSION

THE BIRTH that we celebrate at Christmas has been celebrated for thousands of years. Luke tells us that it was first celebrated by shepherds in a field, together with a "great company of the heavenly hosts" (Luke 2:13).

- But if that birth, if God appearing briefly as a baby, was all there was to celebrate, Christmas would not have held our attention the way that it has.

- We celebrate the coming of Jesus because it is a part of a divinely inspired rescue mission. And we know how the mission ends.

Every Sunday, we share the bread and cup of communion and reflect on the words, 'This is my body given for you... This cup is the new covenant in my blood, which is poured out for you" (Luke 22:20). We celebrate the death of Jesus. We see it as punishment for our sin.

- But if that is all it was, if Jesus only died so that God could forgive us and nothing more, we probably would not observe the Lord's Supper as faithfully as we do.

- We celebrate the death of Jesus because it is a part, maybe the most important part, but nevertheless a part, of a divinely inspired rescue mission. And we know how the mission ends.

Three days after His death, Jesus returned to life. Forty days later, He ascended to heaven. Ten days after that, He sent the Holy Spirit to be "Christ in you, the hope of glory" (Col 1:27). And we have Easter, Ascension Day, and Pentecost to commemorate those events.

- But if they reminded us only that Jesus lives forever, that death has no hold on Him, and implied nothing about our own futures, none of those events would comfort us like they do.

- We celebrate the resurrection, ascension, and gift of the Holy Spirit because they are a part of a divinely inspired mission to rescue a lost and dying world. And we know how the mission ends.

> **For God so loved the world that he gave his one and only Son, that whoever believes in him shall not perish but have eternal life.**
> **(John 3:16)**

That is how the mission ends. In fact, as John pointed out in the final book of the Bible, it ends in a never-ending celebration, and the people who are rescued exclaim:

> **Hallelujah! The Lord our God, the Almighty, exercised his royal power!** **(Rev 19:6 CEB)**

> **Now the dwelling of God is with men. . . He will wipe away every tear from their eyes. There will be no more death or mourning or crying or pain, for the old order of things has passed away** **(Rev 21:3,4 NIV84)**

> **Let us rejoice and celebrate, and give him the glory. . .** **(Rev 19:7 CEB)**

PRAYER

Father, as we take the bread and cup of communion, we find ourselves celebrating the whole story of Jesus—from His miraculous birth to His purposeful death, resurrection, ascension, and even to His presence among us through the Holy Spirit. We are grateful that the life He lived as a man has in some amazing way made it possible for us to one day live with Him forever. So, we celebrate, and we pray in the precious name of Jesus. Amen.

MORE TO CONSIDER

What do you celebrate about the birth of Jesus? As noted above, there are many things from which to choose.

95

MARRIED TO CHRIST

I N 2ND CORINTHIANS, the apostle Paul said that he wanted to present the Christians of Corinth "as a chaste virgin to Christ" (2 Cor 11:2). In the book of Revelation, John pictured the church as a bride that had "made herself ready" for "the wedding banquet of the Lamb" (Rev 19:7). The writers of the New Testament saw marriage as a fitting metaphor for the relationship between Christ and His followers. And that makes sense because a good marriage, like a saving relationship with Christ, is consummated by a covenant that is an act of the will and is based on a love that transcends feelings. Jesus had such a love.

It has been said that we understand the makeup of things best when we see them lying in pieces. And if ever love was laid bare before our eyes, it was when the Son of God hung on a cross. There, we see that above all else love means sacrifice. In the book, *The Reason for God*,[1] Timothy Keller points out that in all loving relationships, "Both sides must say to the other, 'I will adjust to you. I will change for you. I'll serve you even though it means sacrifice for me.'" Jesus said, "Greater love has no one than this, that he lay down his life for his friends" (John 15:13). John wrote, "This is how we know what love is: Jesus Christ laid down his life for us" (1 John 3:16). The greatest love that we will ever know demanded the greatest sacrifice that was ever made—the broken body and shed blood of God in the flesh.

The cross also reveals a love that is unconditional. There was no "quid pro quo" on the cross. Jesus did not expect anything in return.

- He loves us when we pray and study His Word and work to further His kingdom.

- And He loves us when we judge others unfairly, fail to do the good thing that is right in front of our eyes, or even nail Him to a cross and stand by as He dies for our sin.

- 'Father forgive them, he prayed, for they do not know what they are doing" (Luke 23:34).

If you are taking communion today, you are in a sense married to Christ. You have bound yourself to God in a covenant that is built upon sacrificial and unconditional love. And you can look forward to 'the wedding banquet of the Lamb."

PRAYER

Our Heavenly Father, we know that you are love. And it is love that gives meaning to life. We thank for the love that Jesus demonstrated on the cross. The bread and cup are reminders of His sacrifice. May our love for you be like His love for us. Amen.

MORE TO CONSIDER

Can you think of other scriptures that use marriage as a metaphor for the relationship between Christ and His followers? What about Ephesians 5:22-23 or Matthew 9:15? Considering these and the scriptures mentioned above, does it make sense for Christian couples to take communion during their wedding to show that God is at the center of their marriage?

---

[1]Timothy Keller, *The Reason for God* (New York: Penguin Group, 2008), 49.

96

OUR HOPE AND PEACE

YOU CAN THINK of hope as made up of equal parts of expectation and desire. One may expect something but not desire it. You may be expecting a snowstorm or expecting a hard day at work, but you probably do not desire them. On the other hand, you may desire something but not expect it. You may desire a knock on your door from the *Publisher's Clearing House* telling you that you have won 1,000 dollars a week for life, or you may desire a nice vacation on a tropical island, but you may not have reason to expect it.

Hope is the happy combination of expectation and desire. On the first Christmas Eve, Mary had expectation, because she was expecting a child. And she had desire because that child was to be the promised Savior of the world. On that first Christmas Day, there at last was real hope for the world. He was solid hope that you could pick up and feel warm in your arms. He was the hope that came with the prophecies of old and the promise of God's angel. He was the hope of the world. He is our hope.

Peace is the subject of many a Christmas card and Christmas carol. After all, the message of the angels was 'Glory to God in the highest heaven, and on earth peace to those on whom his favor rests" (Luke 2:14). He came as the Prince of Peace. We usually think of peace as the absence of conflict, but there is another kind of peace. It is really a deeper and more difficult kind of peace, for it is the internal peace which makes the absence of conflict possible. Peace on earth is impossible unless it first dwells in the human heart.

When Jesus healed someone, He often said to them "Go in peace" (Luke 8:48). When He appeared to the Apostles after the resurrection, His greeting was often, "Peace be with you" (John 20:21). What did He mean by peace? On one occasion He said: "Peace I leave with you; my peace I give you. I do not give to you as the world gives. Do not let your hearts be troubled and do not be afraid" (John 14:27). There is a good definition of the peace that Jesus brought—do not let your hearts be troubled and do not be afraid. Again, He said: "I have told you these things, so that in me you may have peace. In this world you will have trouble. But take heart! I have overcome the world" (John 16:33). The peace that Jesus gives is the confidence that He has overcome the world. It is the true starting place. It is peace in the human heart. It is our promise, our hope.

Christmas reminds us of hope, that happy mixture of expectation and desire, and peace, that internal calm that reflects a fearless and untroubled heart. But you cannot separate the life of Christ into discreet parts. It is all one. Latent in the baby, just waiting to happen were His life and teaching, His miracles, His suffering and death, His resurrection, His ascension, and His place at the right hand of God. In the Christmas season, we celebrate His birth, but without all the rest it means nothing. So, we also celebrate His death, for by His death He brought hope and peace.

PRAYER

Our Father, we thank you for the birth of Jesus because He is among other things hope and peace. But we thank you even more for the death of Jesus, because He is worthy not only of our admiration but of our worship. Amen.

MORE TO CONSIDER

What is the hope of Christmas? Does it bring you peace?

97

WHAT CHILD IS THIS?

I n the days leading up to Christmas, the thoughts of Christians around the world turn to the birth of Jesus. We sing *"Joy to the world, the Lord has come"*[1] and *"Silent night, holy night, all is calm, all is bright,"*[2] and the farthest thing from our minds is an angry crowd shouting "Crucify him! Crucify him!" (Luke 23:21). We sing *"O come, let us adore Him"*[3] and blindly ignore the obvious—that we are a lot like those who mocked, not adored Him, as He hung on a cross and died for our sin. The carols we sing at Christmas direct our attention to the wonder of Jesus' birth, not the suffering He will later endure or the sin that made it necessary.

But in 1865, William Chatterton Dix wrote a Christmas carol that addresses both. Set to the tune of a 16th century folk song,[4] its title poses the question, *What Child Is This?* And verse one of the carol answers that question with the familiar refrain[5]:

> This, this is Christ the King,
> whom shepherds guard and angels sing;
> Haste, haste to bring him laud,
> The Babe, the Son of Mary.

You have probably never heard the original second verse, because it is omitted from modern versions of the carol. Its lyrics pivot from Bethlehem to Calvary and proclaim:

Nails, spear shall pierce Him through,
the cross be borne for me, for you.
Hail, hail the Word made flesh,
The Babe, the Son of Mary.

The story of Jesus is bigger than the story of His birth. It begins long before His birth when man's sin necessitated His coming. It includes a brutal crucifixion and miraculous resurrection. And it continues today as we retell the story and await His second coming.

So, in addition to celebrating His birth at Christmas, we take the Lord's Supper in remembrance of His death, when the New Covenant grace that we depend on as sinners became a reality. And in anticipation of His return, when we will once again sing, *"Joy to the world, the Lord has come. Let earth receive her king."*

PRAYER

Father, we thank you for Jesus, who in a manger was laid, and on a cross was nailed, and whose Spirit resides in those who follow Him. We are grateful that "The Word became flesh and made his dwelling among us" (John 1:14). And we take the bread and cup, symbols of his body and blood, in remembrance of "the One and Only who came from the Father full of grace and truth" (John 1:14). What child is this? He is our Lord and Savior Jesus Christ, in whose name we pray. Amen.

MORE TO CONSIDER

What do your favorite Christmas hymns say about Jesus? If they are only focused on the nativity, what can you do to remind yourself of the whole story of Jesus? How do you answer the question, "What child is this?"

---

[1]*Joy to the World!*, Isaac Watts. *The Hymnal for Worship and Celebration*. Word Music, Waco, 1986, 125.

[2]*Silent Night! Holy Night!*, Joseph Mohr. *The Hymnal for Worship and Celebration*. Word Music, Waco, 1986, 147.

[3]*O Come, All Ye Faithful*, John Francis Wade. *The Hymnal for Worship and Celebration*. Word Music, Waco, 1986, 145.

[4]*Greensleeves*, a love song referred to in Shakespeare's *Merry Wives of Windsor*.

[5]See https://www.hymnsandcarolsofchristmas.com/Hymns_and_Carols/what_child_is_this_version_1.htm.

98

THE ADORATION
OF THE CHRIST CHILD

THE *ADORATION OF THE CHRIST CHILD* is a 500-year-old painting in the Metropolitan Museum of Art.[1] To quote a 14th-century mystic, its most compelling feature is a "great and ineffable light" emanating from the baby Jesus—a visual reminder that He is the light of the world. An angel on Mary's right and the shepherd in the center of the painting appear to have Down syndrome. The Christ of Christmas—the painting seems to say—is for everyone.

In another painting with the same name,[2] Italian artist Sandro Botticelli pictures the Virgin Mary kneeling in adoration of her Son, while Joseph sleeps and two shepherds on the baby's right hold a sacrificial lamb, foreshadowing Christ's own role as our sacrificial lamb.

David Maitland Armstrong and his daughter, Helen, designed a stained-glass window,[3] also called the *Adoration of the Christ Child*. It was built in 1896 for Faith Chapel in Jekyll Island, Georgia and can still be seen there today. At first glance, it appears to depict three wise men bringing gifts to the newborn Savior. A closer inspection, however, reveals that one of the "wise men" is a Roman soldier, with a sword at his side, and another is offering the future King of the Jews a crown of thorns.

These works remind us that Jesus was no ordinary baby and that it is hard to think about the incarnation without considering the crucifixion.

Adoration of the Christ Child Sketches. The shading denotes elements that are referred in the text. The top sketch is of the painting by Sandro Botticelli; the middle sketch's painter is unknown; the bottom sketch is of the stained-glass window of David and Helen Armstrong. See the footnotes for links to the full-color art.

- The child that was wrapped in swaddling clothes was later stripped of His clothes and made to wear a crown of thorns.

- The baby we imagine lying in a wooden manger was later nailed to a wooden cross.

- And the one who was adored by shepherds and wise men was—in the end—rejected, as He died to save us from our sin.

Whether though art, or music, or literature, Christians have always found ways to express their adoration of Christ. We do so around the Lord's Table, using simple symbols of His broken body and shed blood—the bread and cup of communion.

PRAYER

Father, bless each person as they reflect upon your Son—upon His virgin birth and life without sin, upon the cruelty surrounding His death on a cross and the life-changing consequences of His sacrifice for us. We know that these are the things that make your Kingdom accessible to us, both here in the present and in eternity to come. So, we thank you for the Christ of Christmas and for the Christ of Calvary, in whose name we pray. Amen.

MORE TO CONSIDER

We are not all artists, but we share a common admiration of Jesus. In what ways do you express your adoration of God's Son?

---

[1]Artist unknown, A follower of Jan Joest of Kalkar, *The Adoration of the Christ Child*, 1515, oil on wood, The Met Fifth Avenue, New York, accessed August 16, 2023, https://www.metmuseum.org/art/collection/search/436781.

[2]Sandro Botticelli, *The Adoration of the Christ Child*, c1500, oil on panel, *The Museum of Fine Arts*, Houston, Texas, May 25, 2021, https://catchlight.blog/2021/05/25/botticellis-adorationof-the-christ-child/.

[3]David Maitland Armstrong and Helen Maitland Armstrong, *The Adoration of the Christ Child*, 1896, stained-glass window, Faith Chapel in Jekyll Island, Georgia, accessed August 16, 2023, https://www.jekyllisland.com/history/sites/faith-chapel/.

99

CHRISTMAS

THERE IS NO greater contrast than that of Christmas and communion, the manger and the cross, the beautiful baby and the broken man. The dramatic distinction between the brightest light and the deepest darkness, the farthest place and the nearest point, and the coldest chill and the hottest heat in no way compare. Christmas is peace and quiet and gentleness and hope. We sing:

- *Silent Night! Holy Night! All is calm...*[1]

- *O Little Town of Bethlehem, how still we see thee lie...*[2]

- *The world in solemn stillness lay to hear the angels sing...*[3]

- *What child is this who laid to rest on Mary's lap is sleeping...*[4]

Christmas is a time of peace and quiet, of hope and promise, and sweetness and innocence.

The Lord's Supper reminds us that Mary's baby boy grew up, and we hung Him on a cross. He was still as good as He was as a baby and as innocent, but the world did not want what He had to offer. The peace that the manger promised would come at great cost. His death was a loud ugly thing. "Crucify him!" (Matt 27:22). "Let him save Himself!" (Luke 23:35). When God so loved the world that He gave His only son, He not only gave Him to Mary and to the world, but He gave Him over to the hands

243

of wicked men like us. They took their hate and guilt out on Him, and He took it in—He took ours in too. That is why He came into the world.

He would rise from the dead, of course, and ascend to be with the Father, but between His gentle birth and the sweet victory of resurrection was the rowdy roar of the crowd and the bloody whip and bloody crown and bloody spear and bloody nails. So, we pause amid peace on earth, good will to men and remember the cost of peace and the meaning of good.

PRAYER

Lord, we never want to forget the cost of our forgiveness or the reason for our hope, so we remember this morning with the loaf and the cup. Amen.

MORE TO CONSIDER

Think about your favorite Christmas carols. What are your favorites? Do any of them allude to the later events in Jesus' life?

---

[1]*Silent Night! Holy Night!*, Joseph Mohr. *The Hymnal for Worship and Celebration.* Word Music, Waco, 1986, 147.

[2]*O Little Town of Bethlehem*, Phillips Brooks. *The Hymnal for Worship and Celebration.* Word Music, Waco, 1986, 141.

[3]*It Came upon the Midnight Clear*, Edmund H. Sears. *The Hymnal for Worship and Celebration.* Word Music, Waco, 1986, 128.

[4]*What Child Is This?*, William C. Dix. *The Hymnal for Worship and Celebration.* Word Music, Waco, 1986, 137.

100

EASTER

T SEEMS INCONGRUOUS to be experiencing the Lord's Supper on Easter. There is something warm and fresh and hopeful about Easter. It is eggs and bunnies, pastel colors and paper grass, jellybeans, candy eggs, and chocolate. It is sweetness, light, and life. It is about the resurrection of Jesus. But the Lord's Supper is about His death. There is no sweetness in the un-raised bread and little refreshment in the sip of juice. It does not fit Easter.

When Jesus established the Lord's Supper in the upper room during the Passover meal, He knew that He was going to die, and He knew that He would be raised from the dead. Strangely He did not give the Apostles a hard roll or a pebble to symbolize the rock that was rolled away from the tomb or to remind them of the saying: "He is not here. He is risen" (Matt 28:6). It was not the resurrection they were to intentionally remember in a special meal. He gave them the loaf and the cup to remember His death.

You see, the purpose of Christ's coming was fulfilled in His death. He came to die. He lived under the shadow of the cross. It is by His death that our sins are forgiven. Redemption, reconciliation, propitiation, salvation—all the great theological truths and practical realities of our faith are related to His death. Even our resurrection is not dependent on His resurrection, but on His death. That is why He could say triumphantly on the cross, "It is finished" (John 19:30).

What purpose is served by the resurrection? Why should we celebrate

Easter? The joy of Easter is that the resurrection proves that what we believe about His death was true. So as incongruous as it must be, on a bright and happy Easter day, we must pause to reflect on the saddest and ugliest day in human history—the day that Jesus died.

> While they were eating, Jesus took bread, and when he had given thanks, he broke it and gave it to his disciples, saying, "Take and eat; this is my body." Then he took a cup, and when he had given thanks, he gave it to them, saying, "Drink from it, all of you. This is my blood of the covenant, which is poured out for many for the forgiveness of sins." (Matt 26:26-28)

PRAYER

Lord, thank you for the resurrection of Jesus and the hope that it holds for us. We believe that when He overcame His death, He also overcame our deaths and because He rose, so shall we. But we also understand that it was not primarily in His resurrection that He was victorious, but in His death. So, we thank you as we remember that He died for us. Amen.

MORE TO CONSIDER

Can you explain the relationship between the death and resurrection of Jesus? What did His death accomplish? What did His resurrection prove?

101

THANKSGIVING

THERE IS A SHORT PHRASE that appears in all the Biblical accounts of the Lord's Supper. It almost sounds like a ritual. It is easy to read over it without seeing it. Without it, Matthew's Gospel reads like this:

> While they were eating, Jesus took bread and broke it and gave it to his disciples, saying, "Take and eat; this is my body." Then he took a cup, and gave it to them, saying, "Drink from it, all of you. This is my blood of the covenant, which is poured out for many for the forgiveness of sins. I tell you, I will not drink of this fruit of the vine from now on until that day when I drink it anew with you in my Father's kingdom."
>
> (Matt 26:26-29)

Mark's Gospel reads like this without it:

> While they were eating, Jesus took bread and broke it, and gave it to his disciples, saying, "Take it; this is my body." Then he took the cup and offered it to them, and they all drank from it." (Mark 14:22-23)

Luke's Gospel reads like this without it:

> After taking the cup, he said, "Take this and divide it among you. For I tell you I will not drink again of the fruit of the vine until the kingdom of God comes." And he took bread and broke it, and gave it to them, saying, "This is my body given for you; do this in remembrance of me." (Luke 22:17-18)

Paul's reference in 1 Corinthians would read like this:

> For I received from the Lord what I also passed on to you: The Lord Jesus, on the night he was betrayed, took bread, and broke it and said, "This is my body, which is for you; do this in remembrance of me." In the same way, after supper he took the cup, saying, "This cup is the new covenant in my blood; do this, whenever you drink it, in remembrance of me." For whenever you eat this bread and drink this cup, you proclaim the Lord's death until he comes. (1 Cor 11:23-26)

Do you know the two words that are left out of each of these passages? They are *gave thanks.*

At His last meal, as He was preparing to lay down His life, He gave thanks. Some of the prayers are ritualistic, but not the one that Paul mentions in 1 Corinthians. This was new ground. It came at the end of the meal, after the Passover lamb had been eaten. Nothing was supposed to be eaten after the Passover, but this was a new day. After the second cup of the Passover meal, after the Passover lamb had been eaten, after the Jews were not to eat any more solid food for the rest of the day, Jesus took bread and the fruit of the vine and gave thanks. The bread was His body, soon to be abused and hung on the cross until dead. The juice was His blood, soon to stain the cross and puddle in the dust. But He gave thanks, because with His death and resurrection He would win the world back to God. Given His example, there is hardly a situation in which we should not give thanks.

PRAYER

For food in a world where many walk in hunger; for faith in a world where many walk in fear; for friends in a world where many walk alone; we give you thanks, O Lord. Amen.[1]

MORE TO CONSIDER

List the things that you are most thankful for. What on your list would be appropriate to thank God for when participating in the Lord's Supper?

---

[1]Author unknown.

102

NEW YEAR'S DAY

S THE YEAR comes to an end, it is estimated that roughly half of us will look back on the last year and make a New Year's resolution.[1] It is a tradition as old as man himself. The Babylonians are believed to have started it over 4000 years ago. And the Romans continued the tradition, and added a mythical god named Janus, who had two faces looking in opposite directions so he could see into the past and into the future at the same time.

The intersection of the past and the future, when the clock strikes midnight on the last day of the year, is what the world's oldest holiday is all about. And here is how it is somewhat like the Lord's Supper. In a letter to the Corinthians, Paul wrote:

> For I received from the Lord what I also passed on to you: The Lord Jesus, on the night he was betrayed, took bread, and when he had given thanks, he broke it and said, "This is my body, which is for you; do this in remembrance of me." In the same way, after the supper he took the cup, saying, "This cup is the new covenant in my blood; do this, whenever you drink it, in remembrance of me."   (1 Cor 11:23-25)

That is the past—a bodily sacrifice that builds a bridge between God and us. But Paul goes on to say, "For whenever you eat this bread and drink this cup, you proclaim the Lord's death until he comes" (1 Cor 11:26). And that is the future—the uniting of God and His people in the kind of family that Jesus died to make possible.

The celebration, of course, is recurring, just like the celebration of the New Year, and takes place every time we come around the Lord's Table to proclaim the Lord's death.

Prayer

Not much has really changed since Paul's letter to the Corinthians. You remain "the Alpha and the Omega... the one who is, and who was, and who is to come" (Rev 1:8). When we look back in time, as Jesus instructed us to do, we still see our sin, His sacrifice, and your willingness to surrender your Son for our well-being. And when we look forward in time, as Paul suggested to the Corinthians, we see life after death, a new and perfect body to live it in, and Jesus preparing a place for us, so that where He is, we also may be. Our prayer this morning is to spend our eternity in your presence. Amen.

More to Consider

Take some time to think about your past relationship with God and what you want your future relationship to be. If there are things that you regret, plan the necessary steps to correct them.

---

[1]Sarah Davis and Alena Hall, "New Year's Resolutions Statistics 2023," Forbes, March 9, 2023, https://www.forbes.com/health/mind/new-years-resolutions-statistics/.

103

INDEPENDENCE DAY

ON JULY 2ND, 1776, the Second Continental Congress approved a resolution declaring independence from Great Britain. And on the following day, John Adams, who later became the country's 2nd President, wrote this in a letter to his wife Abigail: "The second day of July 1776 will be the most memorable" day "in the history of America. ... It ought to be commemorated as the Day of Deliverance by solemn acts of devotion to God Almighty."[1] As it turns out, Adams was basically right, but:

- The final version of the Declaration was not ratified until July 4th, the date we celebrate.

- The 4th was not made a national holiday until 1870, almost 100 years later.

- And independence was not really achieved until thousands had sacrificed their lives in the Revolutionary War.

In the 2nd chapter of Hebrews, it is noted that Jesus shared our "humanity so that by his death he might break the power of him who holds the power of death—that is, the devil— and free those who all their lives were held in slavery by their fear of death" (Heb 2:14-15). Like those who purchased our political freedom with their lives, Jesus purchased our freedom from the power and fear of death with His life. So, what John Adams said about Independence Day can be said—to an even greater extent—about the day of Jesus' death: "It ought to be commemorated as the Day of Deliverance, by solemn acts of devotion to God Almighty."

That is what you do when participating in the Lord's Supper:

- You take bread and remember that Jesus' body "was given for you" (Lk 22:19).

- You drink some juice and remember that it represents "his blood, which was poured out for you" (Lk 22:20).

And in the process, you are reminded:

- Of the seriousness of your sin,

- Of the magnitude of Jesus' sacrifice,

- Of the remarkable love of God,

- And of the amazing gift of life everlasting and independence from the power and fear of death.

PRAYER

Father, "Death has been swallowed up in victory" (1 Cor 15:54). And we can face it without fear because of Jesus. His death secured the grace we so desperately need. And we are ever grateful and mindful of His sacrifice, for which we thank you in His name. Amen.

MORE TO CONSIDER

What is the best way you have found to commemorate the independence God has bought for you?

---

[1]David McCullough, *John Adams* (New York: Simon & Schuster, 2001), 130.

104

Communion for Children

HE STORY of the origin of communion goes back thousands of years (about 3500) and it is related to several famous Bible stories that most children know very well. Think about these three people and their stories: Joseph, Moses, and Jesus.

In the story of Joseph, his brothers were jealous of him and sold him into slavery. He was taken to Egypt, but he was so hard working and honest and faithful to God that he became the second most powerful man in Egypt. Years later, his father and eleven brothers and their families were starving because there was no rain and they could grow no food. Joseph told them who he was, forgave them, and invited them to come and live in Egypt, where there was plenty of food. After a few hundred years, Joseph's family grew to be a nation of hundreds of thousands of people. We call them the children of Israel because Joseph's father's name was Israel. We sometimes call them Jews after one of Joseph's brothers Judah. The Egyptian government became afraid of the Jews and made them slaves. That is how the children of Israel got into Egypt and became slaves.

In the story of Moses, we learn how they got out. God called Moses to lead his people out. When the Pharaoh or king refused to let them go, God sent ten plagues, and the tenth was the worst—the death of the first born of everyone in Egypt. Unless Pharaoh obeyed God and released the Jews, the oldest son in every family would die. But God provided the

Jews a way of escape. If they would sacrifice a lamb and paint some of its blood on the door frames of their houses, they would be spared. They were spared and Moses led them out of Egypt. We call this the Exodus, and this event is such an important part of Jewish history that they named a holiday after it—they called it Passover, because the death angel of God passed over them. Every year the Jews celebrated Passover with a meal and a retelling of the story of the Exodus so their children would know the story and never forget it.

Hundreds of years later (about 1500), when Jesus was living, the Jews still celebrated Passover. Jesus was a Jew and at one of the Passover meals, Jesus expanded the meaning of the celebration. He took a piece of the bread and gave thanks for it and said, "take and eat; this is my body," and He took the cup and said "Drink from it ... This is my blood of the covenant which is poured out for many for the forgiveness of sins" (Matt 26:26-29). He did this because He was going to be crucified the next day, was going to be raised from the dead in three days, and was going to ascend into heaven to be with the Father in 40 days.

So, what Moses did in leading the Jews out of Egypt and into the Promised Land is what Jesus did for all people who follow Him. He is the lamb whose blood is shed, and He is the Savior who leads men out of the slavery from sinful lives to a glorious life that never ends. When Jesus gave the apostles the bread and fruit of the vine, He told them to do this in remembrance of Him. That is what communion is. The church has observed it every Sunday from its earliest days. We do the same thing. Remember that Jesus not only came to die for you, but to rise from the dead and live in you so that your life will be filled with His glory.

PRAYER

Father, we are grateful that Jesus said, "Let the little children come to me, and do not hinder them, for the kingdom of heaven belongs to such as these" (Matt 19:13). Amen.

MORE TO CONSIDER

How would you explain the Lord's Supper to your children?

Scripture Index

Genesis
6:5	12
22:8	23

Exodus
6:6	103
12	1, 24
12:26-27	81
20:8	131
20:13	42
21:16	42

Leviticus
4	24
16:8-10	12
24:17	42

Numbers
15:32-36	42

Deuteronomy
19:6	42
31:6	87

Job
3:4	111
9:33-35	39
13:15	218

Psalms
18:2	111
22:1	45
22:14	45
22:16-18	45
51:10-12	152
69:4	45
69:20-21	45, 141
84:11	111

Isaiah
53	27-29
53:4-6	13
53:7	24
53:10	55
53:12	188
55:9	109
64:8	111

Jeremiah
31:31-34	86
31:33	25

Ezekiel
36:27	25

Amos
5:21-23	125

Matthew
4:2	165
4:11	165
4:19	55
5:3	123
5:17	25, 41

5:21-22	42
6:1	125
6:9	179
6:12, 14-15	161
6:33	216
7:21-22	160
8:10	166
9:12	188
10:38	55
13:44	111
19:13	254
21:31	159
22:37	146
22:39	146
26:26	103
26:26-28	80, 88, 94, 178, 222-223, 246
26:26-29	113, 247, 254
26:27-28	104, 129
26:27-30	2
26:28	8
26:39	166
27:17-18	58
27:21-22	58
27:22	243
27:22-25	59
27:25	59
27:35	52
27:40	158
27:42	158
27:45	200
27:46	84
27:51	17
28:6	50, 245
28:7	50
28:20	87

Mark

10:21	55
13:23	166
14:16-26	67
14:22	149
14:22-23	247
14:22-24	2

14:32-36	191
15:34	49, 52, 192, 197

Luke

2:7	165
2:13	227
2:14	233
2:40, 52	165
4:1-13	165
6:46	160
8:48	234
9:23	216
10:21	179
10:25-37	102
12:5	39
14:15-24	114
15:11-32	102
15:19	123
17:32	131
18:9-14	123
19:10	188
22	118
22:14	75, 119, 139
22:14-19	3
22:14-20	18
22:17-18	247
22:17-19	199
22:19	1, 20, 57, 63, 75, 106, 120, 131, 139, 142, 158, 174, 252
22:19-20	16, 25, 72, 83, 101, 135, 143, 160, 167
22:20	24, 86, 120, 139, 142, 174, 227, 252
22:21	139
22:42	55, 172, 173
22:42-44	51
23:21	235
23:26	165
23:34	162, 176, 189, 197, 199, 200, 232
23:35	243
23:36-43	187
23:42	131

23:43	131, 162, 189, 197, 199	16:33	234
		17:20-22	212
23:46	197, 200	17:22-23	149, 150
		19:25-27	189
John		19:26-27	189, 197, 200
1:11	185	19:28	165, 193, 197, 200
1:14	155, 177, 236	19:28-34	8
1:14-18	177	19:30	195, 197, 200, 245
1:16-17	175	20:19-20, 22	111
1:17	177	20:21	234
1:18	106	20:24-29	212
1:29	11, 12, 23, 24	20:25	53
1:36	110	20:28	50
2:15-16	174	21:25	183
3:7-8	111		
3:16	16, 35, 159, 179, 228	Acts	
4	194	2:2-4	111
4:6	165	2:23	53
5:19	197	2:36-39	59
5:39	97	2:37	219
6:25-33	221-222	2:38	219
6:26	222	2:39	59
6:32-35	193	2:42	126
6:35	110, 194	20:7	3, 214
6:38	166	20:28	32
6:53	108		
6:53-58	222	Romans	
6:54	110	1:17	88
6:55	110, 150	3:23	85
6:60	150	5:8	7, 146, 159
9:5	110	5:9	7, 31, 32
10:11	110	5:19	8
11:33-35	166	6:6-7	22
11:35	166, 174	6:23	42, 115
13:1-5	157	8:21-22	16
13:21	166	8:34	90
13:23	190	10:9	182
14:6	110, 144	11	163
14:10	180	11:22	164
14:13	180	15:11-32	102
14:16	87		
14:27	234	1 Corinthians	
15:5	110	1:13	21
15:13	146, 231	1:18-19	21

2:2	71	2:9-11	172
10-11	3	2:12	39
10:16a	1	3:10	66
10:16b, 17	1		
10:16	33	Colossians	
11	3, 65, 118	1:15	98
11:17	126	1:15-23	98
11:23-25	73-74, 92, 134, 249	1:18-20	89
11:23-26	37, 128, 208, 214, 248	1:19-20	22
11:24	96, 104	1:27	228
11:25	89	2:14	53
11:26c	1		
11:26	1, 10, 74, 82, 89, 90,	1 Thessalonians	
	249	5:13	131
11:27	138		
11:28	96, 115, 137, 151	2 Thessalonians	
11:28-29	126	1:5, 11	123
13:2-3	145		
15:3-6	182	1 Timothy	
15:54	252	1:15	169
		1:16	170
2 Corinthians		2:5-6	18, 40
1:3-4	142	3:16	181
5:17	148		
5:21	83	Titus	
11:2	231	2:14	7
Galatians		Hebrews	
2:10	131	2:14-15	251
2:20	22	2:17	17, 166, 173, 174
3:13	83	4:12-13	111
5:24	22	4:15	166, 174
6:14	21	9:14	32
		9:15	17, 86
Ephesians		10:19-20	17
1:7	31, 32	12:2	vii, 22, 167, 168
2:8	176		
2:13	32	James	
		1:23	111
Philippians		2:19	19
2:5, 8	21	4:17	131
2:5-8	170		
2:5-9	166	1 Peter	
2:5-11	171, 182	1:8	38

1:18-20	32	4:21	145
2:24	14, 52	5:3	145
5:8	111		
		Revelation	
1 John		1:4	106
1:7	32	1:8	250
2:2	7	5:12	24, 124
3:16	111, 231	19:6	228
4:2	165	19:7	111, 228, 231
4:8	159, 160	19:9	113
4:9-10	146	20:14	111
4:10	160	21:3, 4	228
4:16	159, 160	21:6	111
4:18	39